The Fortunate

Ten great writers highlight how we created free and affluent societies

Peter Francis Fenwick

Foreword by David Kemp

Connor Court Publishing

Published in 2022 by Connor Court Publishing Pty Ltd

Connor Court Publishing Pty Ltd
PO Box 7257
Redland Bay QLD 4165
sales@connorcourt.com
www.connorcourt.com
Phone 0497-900-685

Printed in Australia

ISBN: 9781922815118

Front cover design: jbacha

To the future: to my grandchildren —

Max, Zoe, and Lucas; and to young people everywhere.

May you discover wisdom from these great minds,

and learn how to create your own wonderful world.

Also by Peter Francis Fenwick:

The Fragility of Freedom: Why Subsidiarity Matters (2014)

Liberty at Risk: Tackling Today's Political Problems (2016)

Contents

Foreword

Can our ideals be achieved, and our dreams given reality?

That depends of course on what they are. It also depends on self-knowledge and an understanding of how the world works. With such understanding we can test the realism of our objectives and can plan to achieve them. Without such understanding, our efforts will likely prove futile.

But does anyone understand human nature and how the world works? Are the cynics right when they identify the selfish pursuit of status, wealth and power as the keys to success, or is there another way?

Human lives through most of time have been consumed with efforts to survive in a world of selfish power-seeking, and the lives of countless individuals have been collateral damage as the few have succeeded at the expense of the many. Even religions that have sought instead a world of love have frequently been dragged into the maelstrom of power-seeking, and seen their ideals abandoned along the way.

Yet in the last few hundred years humanity seems to have set out on a different path, and the apparent inevitability of poverty, sickness and lawless power has been replaced by a world that is succeeding in abolishing poverty, creating wealth, vastly improving health, and restraining lawless power. Selfish power seeking has not ceased, but a way to the achievement of the ideals and dreams of the many, rather than of the few, seems to have opened before us.

The reason for this step-change in human opportunity is the growth in understanding about how the world works, and in human self-knowledge. This new understanding has empowered the many and made possible the restraint of the selfish few.

Peter Fenwick, in this wonderful collection of short readings, has brought together some brilliant historic and recent contributions that illuminate the understanding that has lifted human institutions and policies to the new plane.

His focus is not on the advances of physical, natural and medical sciences, but on the advances in knowledge, gained through experience and logic, of how lawless power may be restrained, poverty abolished, and wealth created, and how human dignity has been advanced as a result.

The most remarkable and fortunate discovery about how the social world works, made in this recent period of history, is that institutions securing extensive and equal human freedom can lead to unparalleled cultural, social, political and economic advance. The old idea that a small number of the powerful, imposing their will and limited understanding on others, can secure peaceful progress for all, has been shown time and again to be false.

The readings collected by Peter Fenwick are designed to explain why this is so, and they provide an overwhelming case for organising society to maximise the contributions of every person, to welcome and honour the variations in talents and ambitions that exist, to acknowledge and utilise the vast pool of knowledge and values dispersed among the whole population, recognising and understanding the implications for peace and prosperity of the enormous web of relationships in which we are all embedded and live our lives. Only a world guided by the principle of equal personal liberty and peaceful co-ordination by free and informed exchange can fulfill hopes of peaceful progress and avoid oppression.

Peter Fenwick has provided classic essays and modern contexts to illustrate the principles that have been learnt, and the need to keep learning from experience. That it is necessary to continue to work to understand these principles shows that they are, to many, counter-intuitive, and that our immediate environments can readily mislead us down paths that end in the failure of good intentions, and if applied to the wider world, oppression. Truths about human beings and human relations, discerned by experience, careful thought and disciplined research need to be understood.

Anyone who wishes to understand our world and be effective in action will benefit from this excellent volume.

David Kemp

May 2020

David Kemp is an Australian politician and academic. From 1990 to 2004 he was a member of the federal parliament, and from 1996 he was a minister in the Howard government overseeing portfolios including Employment, Education and Environment. Before entering parliament, he was Professor of Politics at Monash University and after leaving parliament was Professor and Vice-Chancellor's Fellow at the University of Melbourne, president of the Liberal Party of Australia (Victorian Division) and a fellow of the Australia and New Zealand School of Government. He is the author of Australian Liberalism - a five-volume history of Australia.

Introduction

Life's good. Much better than it was for my parents and my grandparents. Apparently, lots of people have been beavering away to create the free and prosperous world I now enjoy. I'm one of the fortunate. But I am not alone. Indeed, there are millions of us all over the world.[1]

One hundred years ago, my grandparents raised four children in a 100-square metre weatherboard cottage in Geelong West. There was a dunny in the backyard, a rainwater tank to catch drinking water and a Coolgardie safe to keep food fresh. Wood provided the energy needed to run the household, including a wood stove for cooking, a wood-heated copper pot for washing clothes and a small wood fireplace in the parlour.

On a separate suburban block adjacent to the house, my grandfather grew vegetables to serve the family's everyday needs: in season there were potatoes, onions, tomatoes, broad beans, cabbages, lettuces, carrots, parsnips, swedes, pumpkins, marrows, zucchinis, peas, beans, silver beet, spring onions, rhubarb, parsley, mint and basil. Grandpa used a Daisy air rifle to scare the sparrows off his strawberry patch. There were apple, pear, apricot, quince and walnut trees. At the back of the block, a chook shed housed a few hens, which produced eggs for the family. There was a large family Bible but few other books. Grandpa was a barber and rode his bike to work. The family generated its own entertainment. The boys kicked a football on nearby Baker's Oval, and Uncle Doug went on to play for Geelong in the Victorian Football League.

Compare our own experience. Even on the coldest morning, Jill and I wake to a warm home that is centrally heated. Our toilets are inside; no early morning walk in the chilly, half-light of dawn is required. Our food is stored in a refrigerator. Fresh fruit and vegetables are in plentiful supply from the local supermarket. We wash our clothes in an electric

---

1   See Appendix I One hundred years of growth worldwide.

washing machine - saving 10 hours of housework each week.[2] We travel in comfort by car, protected from rain and wind, while listening to the radio or our choice of music, guided by voiced satellite navigation. We get our news and information from print newspapers, magazines and books, as well as online via the internet. We watch news and current affairs, sport and drama on television. We can even watch sport live from around the world – Olympic Games from Tokyo, Grand Slam Tennis from Wimbledon, World Cup Football from Abu Dhabi. Moreover, National Theatre Live enables us to experience the London stage from our local cinema.

The personal computer has let us become authors of our own content in digital form. We communicate frequently and inexpensively by phone, email and social media. Video calling enables us to enjoy live family events with relatives in Sydney, Chicago and Corseaux on Lake Geneva, or we can send them photos taken on our mobile phones. In the twenty-first century, our work is less physical and more productive, so we have more time for pleasant pursuits. We attend concerts and visit art galleries. We socialise with our friends in cafés and restaurants, at the movies and at clubs where we play tennis and golf. At public sporting events we mingle with tens of thousands of our fellow citizens. We fly interstate and overseas for business and holidays. One hundred years ago, my grandparents had none of this.

Today, Australians are safer, wealthier and live longer than ever before. In the last hundred years, homicide rates have fallen from 2.6 to 1.0 per 100,000, gross domestic product (GDP) per capita has risen from $7,828 to $49,831, and life expectancy has risen from 61.0 years to 83.4 years. Similar changes have occurred in other countries, some even more dramatically. More people were lifted out of poverty in the past one hundred years than in the entire history of humankind. Worldwide, GDP per capita rose from $2,241 to $15,212.[3]

Though it is easy to sneer at national income as a shallow and materialistic measure, it correlates with every indicator of human flourishing... Most obviously, GDP per

2   Pinker (2018) p. 251
3   www.ourworldindata.org.

capita correlates with longevity, health and nutrition. Less obviously, it correlates with richer ethical values like peace, freedom, human rights and tolerance… The citizens of richer countries have greater respect for "emancipative" or liberal values such as women's equality, free speech, gay rights, participatory democracy, and protection of the environment. [4]

What changed to give us this delightful, comfortable, and more civil modern life? Why are we so lucky? Will it last?

Renowned economist and management consultant Peter Drucker advised, "You can't add a cubit to your span, but you can extend your reach by standing on the shoulders of those who have gone before."[5] Let us follow his advice and examine what the great minds of the past had to say about these matters. If we can understand how our free and prosperous society came about, we may be able to enjoy it without feeling guilty, and we can learn how to maintain it against forces that might unwittingly destroy it.

What follows is collection of essays by some of my favourite writers. Here, you will find Frédéric Bastiat wittily demolishing protectionism; Leonard E. Read describing the miracle of the price mechanism; F.A. Hayek analysing sound economic decision-making; Ludwig von Mises explaining how life changes when 'the customer becomes king'; Martin Luther King Jr dreaming of a United States in which its founding principles will apply equally regardless of race; Jonathan Haidt, Meg Wheatley and Peter Murphy warning us about disturbing trends in our society; Matt Ridley reviewing 100 years of communism; and Deirdre McCloskey explaining how the Great Enrichment came about due to a change in rhetoric about liberty and human dignity.

There is a joy in knowledge and a self-confidence that comes with understanding. I hope you find these ideas stimulating, and that you will debate them with your friends and colleagues. If reading them whets your appetite for more, I shall have succeeded.

---

4   Pinker, S. (2018) p. 96
5   I think he may have been reading the Bible at the time. King James version (KJV), Matthew 6:27

1

Free trade makes everyone more prosperous

For centuries, most people lived precarious lives of self-sufficient subsistence, producing their own food, clothes and shelter, entertaining themselves and never moving far from home. Only an elite few thrived. As seventeenth-century philosopher Thomas Hobbes put it, for the rest, life was 'solitary, nasty, brutish and short'. [6] In poor seasons, they starved to death.

In the late eighteenth century, the Scottish economist and philosopher Adam Smith observed that work can be done more efficiently if each task is done by a specialist rather than one person undertaking the whole job. This concept became known as *the division of labour*. It acknowledges that specialisation produces benefits from:

- the improved dexterity that comes from practice and repetition;
- time saved when you do not have to swap between tasks; and
- the opportunity to invent machinery to undertake repetitive tasks.

Being willing to trade with strangers is a peculiarly human trait. It enables us to put Smith's theories into practice. It enables us to specialize, to become better and better at what we do. It   enables us to exchange our products, services and ideas with other people. The more we trade the more opportunities we create. The more we trade the more prosperous we become.

As we become more prosperous, we create a surplus beyond what we

6   Hobbes (1651), Ch. XIII

need to survive. We save and invest that surplus, and the capital created from that saving can be used to improve the productivity of labour. The process is exponential. Subsequent generations inherit from the accumulated output and ideas of those who have gone before.

We flourish in urban settings, where we increase our opportunities to interact, create networks and exchanges with our fellow humans. In addition to all its other benefits, the internet increases the effect of urbanisation. It facilitates the exchange of products, services and ideas between hundreds of thousands of collaborators all over the world. We no longer must live in the same city or meet intermittently at conferences and exhibitions to enable us to trade or communicate. We can be in touch any time, and all the time.

And now something that is not at all obvious – nineteenth century British economist David Ricardo's theory of comparative advantage. Ricardo's brilliant insight is that exchange can work positively in both parties' favour even if one party is better at making both objects! Let's assume I have an employee who is a brilliant computer programmer, much better than I am. She also makes a better cup of coffee. Ricardo advised that it is better if she writes the programs – the higher-valued task - and I make the coffee. Likewise, the surgeon is better to do more surgery and leave the sterilization of her instruments to someone with lesser skills – even if she could do that job three times faster. The principle applies to nations, too. Free trade between nations increases the prosperity of both.

Nonetheless, the concept of free trade is not easy to grasp. Protectionism is always popular with the general public and those with vested interests. They believe that products and services should be created locally in order that jobs can be preserved. They fail to consider that the workers are also customers, and that the products and services that their fellow citizens need are then more expensive and probably of a poorer quality. They see the immediate benefit for the few. They do not foresee the long-term detriment for the rest.

Politicians often take advantage of this ignorance. They interfere in the market to save failing businesses in order to win popular approval and subsequently votes. Their reasoning is that they are saving jobs. In the short term, for the workers affected, that may be true. However, in the long term, the industry will die anyway; the job losses will occur, but later. Young workers are enticed into apprenticeships in industries with no future. Workers aged in their thirties or forties, who could have transferred to some other jobs and industries, may find no such opportunities a decade later.

Propping up industries that will become obsolescent diverts funds from other investment opportunities. Consider, for instance, how much better the funds might be used to increase productivity by improving infrastructure or education; or by reducing taxes, thereby facilitating investment in productive businesses. Capital is best in the hands of entrepreneurs. As the Austrian economist Ludwig von Mises advised: "There is no record of an industrial innovation contrived and put into practice by bureaucrats." [7]

In England, early in the nineteenth century, restrictions were placed on the importation of agricultural products. These benefited the land-owning gentry and disadvantaged the poor. By doing so, the gentry received higher financial yields from their lands while the poor paid more for their food. After a concerted political effort by the Anti-Corn Law League, led by Richard Cobden and John Bright, the Corn Laws were repealed in 1846 and resulted in lasting economic benefits for the nation.

Something similar happened one hundred years later. Regulations prohibited the importation of birds and eggs into England. Local poultry from scrawny fowls was expensive.

At the end of the Second World War, former flying ace, Antony Fisher thought he might go into politics, but Professor Hayek advised him to make some money in business and then start a think tank to change public opinion. So that is what he did.

Fisher observed that Americans were eating cheap poultry from plump

---

7   Ludwig von Mises, Liberty & Property. Essay 4.

chickens. In 1952, flouting the law, he brought 24 fertilised White Rock eggs, disguised as Easter eggs, into the country in his hand luggage. From these, he established England's first battery cage chicken farm, Buxted Chickens, using intensive farming techniques learned from colleagues at Cornell University. The result was a dramatic change in Britain's eating habits. By 1964, Fisher became Europe's biggest chicken farmer, producing 500,000 birds a week.

Using the wealth from his chicken business, he created the Institute of Economic Affairs (IEA) which led to the creation of the Atlas Network. Today the Atlas Network partners with over 500 economic think tanks in nearly 100 countries around the world.

Writing about Fisher recently, Perth entrepreneur and founder of the Mannkal Economic Education Foundation, Ron Manners AO, said:

> *Anyone can break some crazy law, clever people can change such a law, however it takes a genius to abolish a crazy law and leave behind a lasting benefit.* [8]

Free trade is the ideal. It makes everyone more prosperous. To counter the ever-present desire for protectionism, countries negotiate free trade agreements (FTAs) with their trading partners. Invariably, these are multi-page documents that set out arrangements in minute detail, taking months to draft, and protecting vested interests as nations seek to negotiate special deals to protect their local markets.

The term 'free trade agreement' is, in fact, an oxymoron. Free trade agreements define what trade is not free, detailing the tariffs payable on the importation of certain goods and the limits on the quantities of others. They are an imperfect, partial solution.

If trade were really free, there would be no need for a legal agreement.

A new FTA between the United States, Canada and Mexico came into effect on 1 July 2020, replacing the former agreement which President Trump asserted was disadvantaging the United States. On 30 December 2018, Australia joined nine other countries to form a trans-

---

8   https://www.mannwest.com/sir-antony-fisher-from-law-breaker-to-knighthood/

Pacific partnership. This agreement includes Australia, Canada, Japan, Mexico, New Zealand, Singapore, Vietnam, Brunei Darussalam, Chile, Malaysia and Peru. It could have included the United States too, but Trump withdrew from negotiations in January 2017. Following Brexit, the United Kingdom's departure from the European Union, Britain continued busily to negotiate new agreements with its European trading partners and the rest of the world. On 17 December 2021, Dan Tehan, Australia's Minister for Trade Tourism and Investment, announced the first of these, a new FTA with Britain that would eliminate tariffs and quotas on 99 per cent of goods.

Yet, once again, free trade is under threat. First, the coronavirus pandemic has led many to raise questions about the extent to which nations need to be self-sufficient in certain essential items, such as pharmaceutical products. Second, the Ricardian ideal is being challenged by the behaviour of the government of the People's Republic of China, which has dishonoured some commercial agreements in order to apply political pressure. Third, there is always the possibility that war might inhibit trading routes, making some products inaccessible.

Reliable supply from our trading partners is necessary if our modern, complex economies are to function effectively. Trust is essential in business relationships. It may be sensible to limit trade with authoritarian regimes whose motives may be political rather than economic and who, consequently, cannot be trusted.

The question of self-sufficiency is a matter of assessing risk. We can mitigate risk in several ways. We can hold inventories. We can diversify our sources of supply. We can purchase alternatives. We can make our own, or at least have the capability to make our own quickly if needed. All these alternatives come at a cost. There are financial, storage and deterioration costs in holding inventories. We will pay more if we do not purchase from the cheapest supplier. There will be consequences if we use inferior products. Nonetheless, such risks can be assessed, and rational decisions made.

The benefits of free trade are as substantial as ever.

Frédéric Bastiat (1801–1850)

Frédéric Bastiat was a French writer and politician – the leading economic journalist of his day, possibly of all time, and a member of the national legislative assembly. His profound, compelling and insightful essays from the 1840s are still inspiring economists today.

Bastiat was orphaned before he was ten, and so he was brought up by his grandfather and aunt. From the age of seventeen Bastiat worked for six years in his uncle's trading business in Bayonne, before moving to Mugron, in the southwest of France, when he inherited his grandfather's farm.

Observing the adverse effects that government regulations were having on businesses in his hometown, Bastiat founded the Bordeaux Association of Free Trade and the French Free Trade Association. He became close friends with Richard Cobden, who was doing similar work with the English Anti-Corn Law League. They corresponded regularly.

In a productive six-year period from 1844, Bastiat's essays explained and developed the theories of Adam Smith and Jean-Baptiste Say, criticised the ideas of Ricardo and Malthus, and exposed the flaws in popular views about protectionism and socialism.

His followers have formed the Bastiat Society, a global network of businesspeople. They believe that widespread prosperity is possible only when a society is free and committed to defending liberty. Its headquarters are in the United States, in Great Barrington, Massachusetts, and it is active throughout the world.

In *Harmonies of Political Economy* (1850), Bastiat showed that the interests of humanity are harmonious and can best be realised within a free society; that what is good for the owner of capital is also good for the worker. In contradiction to Ricardo's gloomy predictions that wages would always fall to subsistence levels, Bastiat's optimistic view that real wages tend to rise in a free market economy has been borne out in practice. For example, wage rates have risen significantly in Eastern Europe since the fall of communism. On the other hand, the more that government intervenes, the more wage rates stagnate, as evidenced in many ostensibly liberal democracies in the past twenty years.

Because as humans we tend to satisfy our wants with minimal effort, so we favour and vote for subsidies and protection. The problem is that this is antagonistic to the wants of those who must pay the resulting higher prices and higher taxes. Production decreases and there is less for everybody. As Bastiat wrote "The state is that great fiction by which everybody tries to live at the expense of everybody else". [9]

Bastiat's style in *Sophismes Economiques* (1848) was to kill fallacies with ridicule. As a master of *reductio ad absurdum* (reduction to the absurd), he would exaggerate. For example, to the suggestion that it would be economically advantageous for the proposed railway from Paris to Madrid to have a forced break at Bordeaux, thereby creating work for the bargemen, porters, commissionaires, hotelkeepers and warehousemen of that city, Bastiat responded that it should also break at Angouleme, Poitiers, Tours, Orleans – in fact, that it should break at all intermediate points, thus creating work for the citizens of all these towns. The result would of course be a railroad of gaps. A negative railway.

Bastiat began his most famous essay, *That Which is Seen and That Which is Not Seen* with an anecdote about a broken window. When a hoodlum throws a brick through the window of the baker's shop, the window

---

9   Devos (2020), p. 138

must be repaired, thereby creating work for the glass maker and the glazier. The baker gets a new shop window. A positive, you might think. Just like rebuilding a city after it has been devastated by war or cyclone. But because the baker must pay for the broken window, he can no longer afford the suit he had planned to purchase. So, the cloth maker, the tailor and the baker are all disadvantaged. The baker has a repaired window as before but does not have the suit. Thus, overall, there are fewer economic goods.

In *That Which is Seen and That Which is Not Seen*, Bastiat defines the basis of good economic policy. He explains the need to consider long-term effects as well as the more immediate, and to consider the effects of policy on the wider community, not just those directly affected. In 1946, Henry Hazlitt built on Bastiat's concepts in *Economics in One Lesson*. This remains one of the clearest expositions of economics ever written. The Mises Institute published a new edition in 2020.

In his open letter to the French parliament – known as the Petition of the Candlemakers – Frédéric Bastiat with delightful wit, demolishes the case for protectionism. Written in 1845, just prior to Cobden's victory with the abolition of the Corn Laws, it is still as fresh, relevant and economically correct as it was when it was penned.

Enjoy Bastiat's little jokes about the sun not shining in England, politicians practising without theory and without principle, and manure being the foundation of all agricultural wealth. But most of all, enjoy the way he uses the arguments of the protectionists to destroy the case for protectionism.

Petition of the Candlemakers

Frédéric Bastiat

A PETITION

From the Manufacturers of Candles, Tapers, Lanterns, sticks, Street Lamps, Snuffers, and Extinguishers, and from Producers of Tallow, Oil, Resin, Alcohol, and Generally of Everything Connected with Lighting.

To the Honourable Members of the Chamber of Deputies.

Gentlemen:

You are on the right track. You reject abstract theories and have little regard for abundance and low prices. You concern yourselves mainly with the fate of the producer. You wish to free him from foreign competition, that is, to reserve the *domestic market* for *domestic industry*.

We come to offer you a wonderful opportunity for your — what shall we call it? Your theory? No, nothing is more deceptive than theory. Your doctrine? Your system? Your principle? But you dislike doctrines, you have a horror of systems, as for principles, you deny that there are any in political economy; therefore, we shall call it your practice — your practice without theory and without principle.

We are suffering from the ruinous competition of a rival who apparently works under conditions so far superior to our own for the production of light that he is *flooding* the *domestic market* with it at an incredibly low price; for the moment he appears, our sales cease, all the consumers turn to him, and a branch of French industry whose ramifications are innumerable is all at once reduced to complete stagnation. This rival, which is none other than the sun, is waging war on us so mercilessly we suspect he is being stirred up against us by perfidious Albion [10] (excellent diplomacy nowadays!), particularly because he has for that haughty island a respect that he does not show for us.

We ask you to be so good as to pass a law requiring the closing of all windows, dormers, skylights, inside and outside shutters, curtains, casements, bull's-eyes, deadlights, and blinds — in short, all openings, holes, chinks, and fissures through which the light of the sun is wont to enter houses, to the detriment of the fair industries with which, we are proud to say, we have endowed the country, a country that cannot, without betraying ingratitude, abandon us today to so unequal a combat.

Be good enough, honourable deputies, to take our request seriously, and do not reject it without at least hearing the reasons that we have to advance in its support.

First, if you shut off as much as possible all access to natural light, and thereby create a need for artificial light, what industry in France will not ultimately be encouraged?

If France consumes more tallow, there will have to be more cattle and sheep, and, consequently, we shall see an increase in cleared fields, meat, wool, leather, and especially manure, the basis of all agricultural wealth.

If France consumes more oil, we shall see an expansion in the cultivation of the poppy, the olive, and rapeseed. These rich yet soil-exhausting plants will come at just the right time to enable us to put to profitable use the increased fertility that the breeding of cattle will impart to the land.

Our moors will be covered with resinous trees. Numerous swarms of bees will gather from our mountains the perfumed treasures that today waste their fragrance, like the flowers from which they emanate. Thus, there is not one branch of agriculture that would not undergo a great expansion.

The same holds true of shipping. Thousands of vessels will engage in

---

10   Bastiat refers to Britain by its archaic name Albion.

whaling, and in a short time we shall have a fleet capable of upholding the honour of France and of gratifying the patriotic aspirations of the undersigned petitioners, chandlers, etc.

But what shall we say of the *specialities* of *Parisian manufacture*? Henceforth you will behold gilding, bronze, and crystal in candlesticks, in lamps, in chandeliers, in candelabra sparkling in spacious emporia compared with which those of today are but stalls.

There is no needy resin-collector on the heights of his sand dunes, no poor miner in the depths of his black pit, who will not receive higher wages and enjoy increased prosperity.

It needs but a little reflection, gentlemen, to be convinced that there is perhaps not one Frenchman, from the wealthy stockholder of the Anzin Company to the humblest vendor of matches, whose condition would not be improved by the success of our petition.

We anticipate your objections, gentlemen; but there is not a single one of them that you have not picked up from the musty old books of the advocates of free trade. We defy you to utter a word against us that will not instantly rebound against yourselves and the principle behind all your policy.

Will you tell us that, though we may gain by this protection, France will not gain at all, because the consumer will bear the expense?

We have our answer ready:

You no longer have the right to invoke the interests of the consumer. You have sacrificed him whenever you have found his interests opposed to those of the producer. You have done so in order *to encourage industry and to increase employment*. For the same reason you ought to do so this time too.

Indeed, you yourselves have anticipated this objection. When told that the consumer has a stake in the free entry of iron, coal, sesame, wheat, and textiles, "Yes," you reply, "but the producer has a stake in their exclusion." Very well, surely if consumers have a stake in the admission of natural light, producers have a stake in its interdiction.

"But," you may still say, "the producer and the consumer are one and the same person. If the manufacturer profits by protection, he will make the farmer prosperous. Contrariwise, if agriculture is prosperous, it will open markets for manufactured goods." Very well, if you grant us a monopoly over the production of lighting during the day, first of all we shall buy large amounts of tallow, charcoal, oil, resin, wax, alcohol, silver, iron, bronze, and crystal, to supply our industry; and, moreover, we and our numerous suppliers, having become rich, will consume a great deal and spread prosperity into all areas of domestic industry.

Will you say that the light of the sun is a gratuitous gift of Nature, and that to reject such gifts would be to reject wealth itself under the pretext of encouraging the means of acquiring it?

But if you take this position, you strike a mortal blow at your own policy; remember that up to now you have always excluded foreign goods *because* and *in proportion* as they approximate gratuitous gifts. You have only *half* as good a reason for complying with the demands of other monopolists as you have for granting our petition, which is in *complete* accord with your established policy; and to reject our demands precisely because they are *better founded* than anyone else's would be tantamount to accepting the equation: $+ \times + = -$; in other words, it would be to heap *absurdity* upon *absurdity*.

Labour and Nature collaborate in varying proportions, depending upon the country and the climate, in the production of a commodity. The part that Nature contributes is always free of charge; it is the part contributed by human labour that constitutes value and is paid for.

If an orange from Lisbon sells for half the price of an orange from Paris, it is because the natural heat of the sun, which is, of course, free of charge, does for the former what the latter owes to artificial heating, which necessarily has to be paid for in the market.

Thus, when an orange reaches us from Portugal, one can say that it is given to us half free of charge, or, in other words, at *half price* as compared with those from Paris.

Now, it is precisely on the basis of its being *semigratuitous* (pardon the word) that you maintain it should be barred. You ask: "How can French labour withstand the competition of foreign labour when the former has to do all the work, whereas the latter has to do only half, the sun taking care of the rest?" But if the fact that a product is *half* free of charge leads you to exclude it from competition, how can its being *totally* free of charge induce you to admit it into competition? Either you are not consistent, or you should, after excluding what is half free of charge as harmful to our domestic industry, exclude what is totally gratuitous with all the more reason and with twice the zeal.

To take another example: When a product — coal, iron, wheat, or textiles — comes to us from abroad, and when we can acquire it for less labour than if we produced it ourselves, the difference is a *gratuitous gift* that is conferred upon us. The size of this gift is proportionate to the extent of this difference. It is a quarter, a half, or three-quarters of the value of the product if the foreigner asks of us only three-quarters, one-half, or one-quarter as high a price. It is as complete as it can be when the donor, like the sun in providing us with light, asks nothing from us. The question, and we pose it formally, is whether what you desire for France is the benefit of consumption free of charge or the alleged advantages of onerous production. Make your choice, but be logical; for as long as you ban, as you do, foreign coal, iron, wheat, and textiles, *in proportion* as their price approaches zero, how inconsistent it would be to admit the light of the sun, whose price is *zero* all day long!

The Petition of the Candlemakers comes from Bastiat's *Sophismes Economiques*, first published in 1845. This translation was done by Arthur Goddard and then slightly edited by François-René Rideau for Bastiat.org. Permission to reprint was granted by FEE.

2

Prices transmit the minimum information needed for the efficient use of economic resources

The key insight of Adam Smith's Wealth of Nations is misleadingly simple: if an exchange between two parties is voluntary, it will not take place unless both believe they will benefit from it. Most economic fallacies derive from the neglect of this simple insight, from the tendency to assume that there is a fixed pie, that one party can gain only at the expense of another.[11]

The miracle of the price mechanism is that when this simple concept is applied universally it coordinates the voluntary transactions of millions of people. Acting in their own best interest they make everyone better off.

When Fenwick Software implements an ERP System,[12] it gets paid for its services and the client gains productive improvements to their business. It is much the same if we buy a dozen eggs from the supermarket. In both cases, the prices need to be set so that the deal is good for both parties.

---

11   Friedman, M. & Friedman, R., (1980) p. 13
12   ERP is short for Enterprise Resource System. It has become the generic term for a commercial business system that embraces all the functions of a business in an integrated way.

Price rises create the incentive for buyers and sellers to use economic resources efficiently.

If there is a scarcity – if there are too few consultants to meet the demand for ERP Systems, or too few eggs to meet the demand for breakfast – then the price of consultants and eggs will rise. We will need to change our plans. The client may seek alternative ways to acquire an ERP System. Perhaps packaged software will replace custom software and fewer consultant hours will be required. Perhaps some people will replace their bacon and egg breakfast with cereal.

Price rises transmit information about scarcity and encourage positive economic reaction. The cause of the price rise is immaterial. No-one needs to know why there are insufficient consultants or eggs. It does not concern us that the consultant shortage is due to universities focusing on training lawyers, or that there has been an epidemic in the chicken industry. Prices efficiently transmit the minimal information and only to those who need to know.

When an item, or a component of manufacture, becomes scarce we will seek alternatives. In this way, maximum benefit is gained from the scarce resource and other resources are brought into play. Alternatively, production may be increased, but this will require increased investment and probably the use of costlier inputs. For instance, we could retrain graduates from other disciplines in information technology and expand the chicken farming industry.

For the price miracle to function properly the principle of private property must apply. As entrepreneurs, we need to be secure in the ownership of our efforts and our risk-taking. Otherwise, there is no incentive for us to respond to shortages.

***

Interest rates are a special case of the price mechanism. They determine the price of money. They transmit information to borrowers and lenders. Higher interest rates encourage us to save. Lower interest rates encourage us to invest. A free market will keep these in equilibrium. The absolute value at which this happens will depend on our time preference – our willingness to delay instant gratification in return for future benefits.

A lower time preference is economically desirable.

When we save money, it can be borrowed by entrepreneurs and invested in capital goods: roads, bridges, ports, mines, factories, warehouses, machinery, scientific research and so on. In the future, we will be able to buy consumer goods such as cars, refrigerators, mobile phones, furniture, carpets, toilets, copper pipes, corrugated iron roofs, carpets, barbecues, our children's education, guitars, shoes, shirts, toys, televisions, whatever, with the money we have saved. This is the normal and proper functioning of an economy. But if the credit comes from our government printing money and not from our savings, then we will not have the funds to afford the consumer goods and the capital investment will have been wasted. That is what causes a recession.

A lower time preference is also socially desirable.

When we focus on the future, we are concerned about our reputation and that of our family and our business. We value trusting relationships. We behave more ethically. We are less likely to be aggressive or to cheat, lie or steal, because the short-term rewards do not compensate for being ostracised socially and in business.

Unfortunately, interest rates – the most important price in our economy – are no longer set by the market. Ever since the First World War, the supply of money has been controlled by governments through their central banks. [13] We are worse off economically and morally for that.

---

13   Rothbard, M.N. (1963/2005)

Leonard E. Read (1898–1983)

Leonard Read was no stranger to hard work. Orphaned at age ten, he worked on the family farm and in the local store. At high school, he earned his keep doing maintenance work on the school's grounds. Read joined the Air Corps in the First World War, survived being sunk off Scotland and, after the war, served for a year in Germany in the army of occupation. Upon his return, Read ran a wholesale business in Ann Arbor, Michigan. During the Depression and the Second World War he held management positions with the United States Chamber of Commerce in San Francisco, Seattle and Los Angeles.

Charismatic, energetic and debonair, Leonard Read was a businessman and a manager. But most of all, he was a moral philosopher. He believed in an individual's rights to life and property; that we should not use force, or threat of force, or fraud to impose our wishes upon others; nor should we hinder or prevent transactions between willing traders; and that no-one, neither private individual nor public agency, should take property from one person for the benefit of another. Consequentially, Read was a trenchant opponent of the New Deal, which he viewed as not only economically inefficient but also morally bankrupt.

By 1946, President Franklin Roosevelt's interventionist policies had become entrenched. The public had come to accept emergency legislation and price, wage and rent controls as the norm. Read recognised that to oppose such deeply held views required changes to public opinion.

He understood that it takes an organization to publish books and pamphlets, to hire speakers, to schedule lectures and to arrange seminars. Encouraged by contacts he had made in the Chamber of Commerce, Read established the Foundation for Economic Education (FEE). Its mission, inspired by the ideas of Albert Schweitzer and Albert Jay Nock, was to spread the philosophy of freedom. Its major activity was seminars in which speakers from FEE would interact with audiences to engage them in debate. The foundation continues to flourish today, inspiring young people to play a role in the creation of a free, fair and prosperous society.

In 1950, Read joined the board of the newly established free market periodical *The Freeman*, which was the forerunner of *National Review*, and in 1954 brought it under the wing of FEE.

Read was an enthusiastic sponsor of Bastiat and Mises. He revived interest in Bastiat's ideas by arranging new translations of *The Law*, *Economic Sophisms*, *Economic Harmonies*, and *Selected Essays in Political Economy*. Ludwig von Mises had arrived in New York in 1940 at the age of 59, with no job, a stranger in a foreign land. Although well known in Europe, his Austrian economics ran counter to the Keynesian ideas that were in vogue at the time. Thus, opportunities were limited. Mises joined FEE as an economic advisor. It provided him with a platform to speak at seminars and publish in *The Freeman*. It also provided secretarial and editorial support for *Human Action*, which was published by Yale University in 1949.

> Leonard Read was a prolific writer and public advocate for freedom. He wrote 29 books. However, he is best remembered for *I, Pencil*, his essay on the price mechanism. His tale about the production of a simple pencil illustrates how free enterprise works. He explains how the price miracle has enabled the collaboration of millions of people, in worldwide supply chains, to produce myriads of things, and how they each prosper by doing their bit without needing to know what the others are doing. Significantly, in this process there is no mastermind, no-one controlling their activities.

I, Pencil
My Family Tree as told to Leonard E. Read

I am a lead pencil – the ordinary wooden pencil familiar to all boys and girls and adults who can read and write.

Writing is both my vocation and my avocation; that's all I do.

You may wonder why I should write a genealogy. Well, to begin with, my story is interesting. And, next, I am a mystery – more so than a tree or a sunset or even a flash of lightning. But, sadly, I am taken for granted by those who use me, as if I were a mere incident and without background. This supercilious attitude relegates me to the level of the commonplace. This is a species of the grievous error in which mankind cannot too long persist without peril. For, the wise G. K. Chesterton observed, 'We are perishing for want of wonder, not for want of wonders.'

I, Pencil, simple though I appear to be, merit your wonder and awe, a claim I shall attempt to prove. In fact, if you can understand me – no, that's too much to ask of anyone – if you can become aware of the miraculousness which I symbolize, you can help save the freedom mankind is so unhappily losing. I have a profound lesson to teach. And I can teach this lesson better than can an automobile or an airplane or a mechanical dishwasher because – well, because I am seemingly so simple.

Simple? Yet, *not a single person on the face of this earth knows how to make me.* This sounds fantastic, doesn't it? Especially when it is realized that there are about one and one-half billion of my kind produced in the U.S.A. each year.

Pick me up and look me over. What do you see? Not much meets the eye – there's some wood, lacquer, the printed labelling, graphite lead, a bit of metal, and an eraser.

Innumerable Antecedents

Just as you cannot trace your family tree back very far, so is it impossible for me to name and explain all my antecedents. But I would like to suggest enough of them to impress upon you the richness and complexity of my background.

My family tree begins with what in fact is a tree, a cedar of straight grain that grows in Northern California and Oregon. Now contemplate all the saws and trucks and rope and the countless other gear used in harvesting and carting the cedar logs to the railroad siding. Think of all the persons and the numberless skills that went into their fabrication: the mining of ore, the making of steel and its refinement into saws, axes, motors; the growing of hemp and bringing it through all the stages to heavy and strong rope; the logging camps with their beds and mess halls, the cookery and the raising of all the foods. Why, untold thousands of persons had a hand in every cup of coffee the loggers drink!

The logs are shipped to a mill in San Leandro, California. Can you imagine the individuals who make flat cars and rails and railroad engines and who construct and install the communication systems incidental thereto? These legions are among my antecedents.

Consider the millwork in San Leandro. The cedar logs are cut into small, pencil-length slats less than one-fourth of an inch in thickness. These are kiln dried and then tinted for the same reason women put rouge on their faces. People prefer that I look pretty, not a pallid white. The slats are waxed and kiln dried again. How many skills went into the making of the tint and the kilns, into supplying the heat, the light and power, the belts, motors, and all the other things a mill requires? Sweepers in the mill among my ancestors? Yes, and included are the men who poured the concrete for the dam of a Pacific Gas & Electric Company hydroplant which supplies the mill's power!

Don't overlook the ancestors present and distant who have a hand in transporting sixty carloads of slats across the nation.

Once in the pencil factory—$4,000,000 in machinery and building, all capital accumulated by thrifty and saving parents of mine—each slat is given eight grooves by a complex machine, after which another machine lays leads in every other slat, applies glue, and places another slat atop—a lead sandwich, so to speak. Seven brothers and I are mechanically carved from this "wood-clinched" sandwich.

My "lead" itself—it contains no lead at all—is complex. The graphite is mined in Ceylon. Consider these miners and those who make their many tools and the makers of the paper sacks in which the graphite is shipped and those who make the string that ties the sacks and those who put them aboard ships and those who make the ships. Even the lighthouse keepers along the way assisted in my birth—and the harbor pilots.

The graphite is mixed with clay from Mississippi in which ammonium hydroxide is used in the refining process. Then wetting agents are added such as sulfonated tallow—animal fats chemically reacted with sulfuric acid. After passing through numerous machines, the mixture finally appears as endless extrusions—as from a sausage grinder-cut to size, dried, and baked for several hours at 1,850 degrees Fahrenheit. To increase their strength and smoothness the leads are then treated with a hot mixture which includes candelilla wax from Mexico, paraffin wax, and hydrogenated natural fats.

My cedar receives six coats of lacquer. Do you know all the ingredients of lacquer? Who would think that the growers of castor beans and the refiners of castor oil are a part of it? They are. Why, even the processes by which the lacquer is made a beautiful yellow involve the skills of more persons than one can enumerate!

Observe the labelling. That's a film formed by applying heat to carbon black mixed with resins. How do you make resins and what, pray, is carbon black?

My bit of metal—the ferrule—is brass. Think of all the persons who mine zinc and copper and those who have the skills to make shiny sheet brass from these products of nature. Those black rings on my ferrule are black nickel. What is black nickel and how is it applied? The complete story of why the center of my ferrule has no black nickel on it would take pages to explain.

Then there's my crowning glory, inelegantly referred to in the trade as "the plug," the part man uses to erase the errors he makes with me. An ingredient called "factice" is what does the erasing. It is a rubber-like product made by reacting rape-seed oil from the Dutch East Indies with sulfur chloride. Rubber, contrary to the common notion, is only for binding purposes. Then, too, there are numerous vulcanizing and accelerating agents. The pumice comes from Italy; and the pigment which gives "the plug" its color is cadmium sulfide.

No One Knows

Does anyone wish to challenge my earlier assertion that no single person on the face of this earth knows how to make me?

Actually, millions of human beings have had a hand in my creation, no one of whom even knows more than a very few of the others. Now, you may say that I go too far in relating the picker of a coffee berry in far off Brazil and food growers elsewhere to my creation; that this is an extreme position. I shall stand by my claim. There isn't a single person in all these millions, including the president of the pencil company, who contributes more than a tiny, infinitesimal bit of know-how. From the standpoint of know-how, the only difference between the miner of graphite in Ceylon and the logger in Oregon is in the *type* of know-how. Neither the miner nor the logger can be dispensed with, any more than can the chemist at the factory or the worker in the oil field—paraffin being a by-product of petroleum.

Here is an astounding fact: Neither the worker in the oil field nor the chemist nor the digger of graphite or clay nor any who mans or makes the ships or trains or trucks nor the one who runs the machine that does the knurling on my bit of metal, nor the president of the company performs his singular task because he wants me. Each one wants me less, perhaps, than does a child in the first grade. Indeed, there are some among this vast multitude who never saw a pencil, nor would they know how to use one. Their motivation is other than me. Perhaps it is something like this: Each of these millions sees that he can thus exchange his tiny know-how for the goods and services he needs or wants. I may or may not be among these items.

No Master Mind

There is a fact still more astounding: the absence of a master mind, of anyone dictating or forcibly directing these countless actions which bring me into being. No trace of such a person can be found. Instead, we find the Invisible Hand at work. This is the mystery to which I earlier referred.

It has been said that "only God can make a tree." Why do we agree with this? Isn't it because we realize that we ourselves could not make one? Indeed, can we even describe a tree? We cannot, except in superficial terms. We can say, for instance, that a certain molecular configuration manifests itself as a tree. But what mind is there among men that could even record, let alone direct, the constant changes in molecules that transpire in the life span of a tree? Such a feat is utterly unthinkable!

I, Pencil, am a complex combination of miracles: a tree, zinc, copper, graphite, and so on. But to these miracles which manifest themselves in Nature an even more extraordinary miracle has been added: the configuration of creative human energies—millions of tiny know-hows configurating naturally and spontaneously in response to human necessity and desire and *in the absence of any human master-minding!* Since only God can make a tree, I insist that only God could make me. Man can no more direct these millions of know-hows to bring me into being than he can put molecules together to create a tree.

The above is what I meant when writing, "If you can become aware of the miraculousness which I symbolize, you can help save the freedom mankind is so unhappily losing." For, if one is aware that these know-hows will naturally, yes, automatically, arrange themselves into creative and productive patterns in response to human necessity and demand—that is, in the absence of governmental or any other coercive masterminding—then one will possess an absolutely essential ingredient for freedom: *a faith in free people*. Freedom is impossible without this faith.

Once government has had a monopoly of a creative activity such, for instance, as the delivery of the mails, most individuals will believe that the mails could not be efficiently delivered by men acting freely. And here is the reason: Each one acknowledges that he himself doesn't know how to do all the things incident to mail delivery. He also recognizes that no other individual could do it. These assumptions are correct. No individual possesses enough know-how to perform a nation's mail delivery any more than any individual possesses enough know-how to make a pencil. Now, in the absence of faith in free people—in the unawareness that millions of tiny know-hows would naturally and miraculously form and cooperate to satisfy this necessity—the individual cannot help but reach the erroneous conclusion that mail can be delivered only by governmental "master-minding."

Testimony Galore

If I, Pencil, were the only item that could offer testimony on what men and women can accomplish when free to try, then those with little faith would have a fair case. However, there is testimony galore; it's all about us and on every hand. Mail delivery is exceedingly simple when compared, for instance, to the making of an automobile or a calculating machine or a grain combine or a milling machine or to tens of thousands of other things. Delivery? Why, in this area where men have been left free to try, they deliver the human voice around the world in less than one second; they deliver an event visually and in motion to any person's home when it is happening; they deliver 150 passengers from Seattle to Baltimore in less than four hours; they deliver gas from Texas to one's range or furnace in New York at unbelievably low rates and without subsidy; they deliver each four pounds of oil from the Persian Gulf to our Eastern Seaboard—halfway around the world—for less money than the government charges for delivering a one-ounce letter across the street!

The lesson I have to teach is this: *Leave all creative energies uninhibited.* Merely organize society to act in harmony with this lesson. Let society's legal apparatus remove all obstacles the best it can. Permit these creative know-hows freely to flow. Have faith that free men and women will respond to the Invisible Hand. This faith will be confirmed. I, Pencil, seemingly simple though I am, offer the miracle of my creation as testimony that this is a practical faith, as practical as the sun, the rain, a cedar tree, the good earth.

I, Pencil was first published in the December 1958 issue of *The Freeman.* Permission to reprint was granted by the Foundation for Economic Education (FEE)

3

Economic decisions are best made by the man on the spot

A funny thing happened in 2020 and 2021. Throughout the world, citizens in many mature democracies surrendered their liberties without a whimper and complied with onerous regulations in response to the coronavirus pandemic. Political leaders enjoyed the sudden thrill of authoritarian power, all the while hiding behind the expert advice of their chief health officers. At both international and local levels, well-developed pandemic plans were abandoned without explanation or justification.[14]

On October 4, 2020, Dr. Sunetra Gupta from Oxford, Dr Jay Bhattacharrya from Stanford, and Dr Martin Kulldorf from Harvard issued their Great Barrington Declaration.

As infectious disease epidemiologists and public health scientists we have grave concerns about the damaging physical and mental health impacts of the prevailing COVID-19 policies, and recommend an approach we call Focused Protection.[15]

Not only was their advice ignored but they were subject to "an onslaught of insults, personal criticism, intimidation and threats."[16] Their colleague, Dr Scott Atlas, suffered a similar fate which he has documented in his memoire *A Plague upon our House*.[17]

---

14   Sabhlok (2020)
15   https://gbdeclaration.org
16   https://www.dailymail.co.uk/debate/article-8899277
17   Atlas (2021)

Our experiences in Melbourne, Australia, were like those in many other cities around the world, but lockdowns and other restrictions lasted longer. Curfews were imposed, keeping us locked in our homes at night. In the daytime we were permitted to venture out for an hour each day, within 5 kilometres of our homes and only for exercise and essential shopping – social or recreational activities were not allowed. Businesses deemed to be non-essential were forced to close, as were schools. We were not allowed to invite extended family, friends, or neighbours into our homes. Families were unable to visit relatives in nursing homes and hospitals. Elective surgery was deferred indefinitely. There was no public entertainment: art galleries, libraries, concert halls, cinemas and sporting venues were all closed. Events were banned, including weddings, funerals and other gatherings. Travel was curtailed. Interstate travel was not permitted for any reason other than those deemed to be essential. International travellers, including students and backpackers, were forbidden to enter the country for study or work. Any Australian resident who happened to be overseas at the time was unable to return. The regulations were enforced uniformly, regardless of the local incidence of the virus.

The expert advice for these regulations came from chief health officers. Significantly, they were not expert in matters of business, sociology, or education. Even their knowledge of medicine was limited. Some had spent most of their working life in administration rather than practicing their profession. They had no way of balancing their decisions by considering the impact on the livelihoods of the owners and workers in the businesses they shut down, the impact on the education and social development of the children unable to go to school, or the impact on the mental health of people denied the opportunity to socialise with family, friends, and workmates. Many of the adverse consequences may be long-term and may not be noticed for years.

Thus, officials with insufficient skill, expertise, knowledge, and data have been making decisions which impact the lives and livelihoods of millions both now and in the future. Their solutions have not addressed the whole problem. They have not taken account of all the factors. They have been sub-optimal, unbalanced, and sometimes punitive. The reasons for arbitrary and inconsistent regulations were never explained. Maybe there were no reasons, just gut feel. Maybe they were not explained because they would not have withstood public scrutiny.

Your average citizen perfectly understands the need for hygiene, to stay at home if unwell, when it is sensible to wear a mask, why it is a good idea to get vaccinated, and so on. Businesses are accustomed to creating safe working environments. Schools care for their students; artists for their audiences. So here is a thought. Maybe we could have achieved the same health outcomes without the negative consequences of mandatory lockdowns if governments had been prepared to provide frequent, detailed, accurate and current information at the local level and then left it to citizens to make their own sensible decisions – in other words if the government shared its information and made recommendations not regulations.

By making it voluntary they may have been more likely to get compliance. When people are treated with respect and given information they can trust they respond positively. Observe that tens of thousands of citizens lined up for tests and vaccinations.

It is time to consider the evidence. International comparative data shows that there was no beneficial association between lockdowns and the incidence of COVID-19 deaths.[18, 19, 20, 21, 22]

It is not simply that lockdowns don't work. We must face the fact that the state is an ineffective institution for the control of a pandemic. Only adult behaviour by informed citizens can resolve such problems.

In the next essay, *The Use of Knowledge in Society,* F.A. Hayek addresses the generic problem of how to make rational economic decisions. Hayek bases his analysis on three profound concepts. First, that not

---

18 Allen (2021)
19 Frijters, Foster and Baker (2021)
20 Agrawal, Cantor, Sood, and Whaley (2021)
21 https://c2cjournal.ca/2021/03/do-lockdowns-make-a-difference-in-a-pandemic/
22 Atlas (2021), p. 298 - 310

all knowledge is scientific; there is also the knowledge of time and place. Second, that knowledge of time and place is held by millions of individuals. Third, data that is aggregated loses nuance.

Hayek explains that sound economic decisions cannot be made centrally by experts or bureaucrats, because they can never have all the knowledge needed. Moreover, they lack transient information about people, local conditions and special circumstances.[23] That is why, in addressing the coronavirus pandemic, we must delegate responsibility to the man on the spot.

For example, you can use population statistics to determine how many vaccine vials are required to vaccinate all Australians over the age of 18 years. But if you want to know how many residents of an aged-care home to vaccinate next week, then you need to know how many missed out last week due to an outbreak of diarrhoea (or some other reason), and whether sufficient nursing staff can be rostered to administer the injections. Similarly, a local real estate agent is likely to have a better idea of the value of your home than the Australian Bureau of Statistics, because they have current knowledge of what buyers are looking for and how much they are prepared to pay. We see this also in the skills of professionals and tradespeople. They make well-founded decisions by drawing on their lifetime of work experience. There is stuff they know that can never be recorded in textbooks, nor taught in a classroom.

In business, managers make decisions every day, varying their processes to meet changes in demand for their products, or the supply of raw materials, or the unexpected failure of a machine, or the unavailability of staff. They are responding to information that is local and immediate. But what about data that is neither local nor immediate? How does the business manager acquire such necessary information with minimal effort?

Hayek's solution is the price mechanism. He extols it as a marvel – one of the greatest triumphs of the human mind. Hayek illustrates the effectiveness of the price mechanism by explaining what happens when,

---

23   That is, the knowledge of time and place

somewhere in the world, a tin mine collapses, or some new opportunity arises for the use of tin. It does not matter which. The price of tin rises and consequently business managers throughout the world must economise on tin or find alternatives. The price system enables the business manager to make decisions without needing to know the cause of the changes in demand. It is a conduit for the minimum information required to make decisions.

The problem for a planned economy is that it does not have a price mechanism. It has no way of allocating scarce resources; no way of making rational economic choices. Mises explained this deficiency one hundred years ago in his paper on economic calculation.[24]

The price mechanism is under-recognised and undervalued, possibly because no-one discovered it and no-one designed it. It facilitates the division of labour upon which our prosperity is based. It enables individuals to choose their employment and to use their knowledge and skills to their own and the community's optimal benefit. The price mechanism enables society to use the knowledge of millions of people to optimise the allocation of scarce economic resources. It is a profound concept. A miracle even. It enables economic decisions to be made by the man, or woman, on the spot.

---

24   Ludwig von Mises, *Economic Calculation in the Socialist Commonwealth, 1920*

F.A. Hayek (1899–1992)

Friedrich August von Hayek was born in Vienna, Austria into a distinguished family of scholars, which included his cousin, the philosopher Ludwig Wittgenstein.

Hayek obtained his doctoral degrees in law and political science from the University of Vienna, where he also participated in Ludwig von Mises' *privatseminar.*

In 1974, Hayek and Gunnar Myrdal were jointly awarded the Nobel Memorial Prize in Economic Sciences 'for their pioneering work in the theory of money and economic fluctuations and for their penetrating analysis of the interdependence of economic, social and institutional phenomena'.

Hayek's academic life was spent mostly at the London School of Economics (1931–50), the University of Chicago (1950–62) and the University of Freiburg (1962–68). He was a pioneer in monetary theory and a leading proponent of classical liberalism.

In 1947, Hayek invited a group of distinguished economists, philosophers and historians – including Frank Knight, Karl Popper, Ludwig von Mises, George Stigler and Milton Friedman – to a meeting at Mont Pelerin in Switzerland, where they agreed to form The Mont Pelerin Society. He remained its president until 1961. The society is still active, continuing to fight for the central values of civilisation: the essential conditions of human dignity and freedom, for freedom of thought and expression, and against the imposition of arbitrary power on the individual and the voluntary group.

Early in his career, Hayek recognised that the spontaneous order of the unplanned free market coordinated human actions efficaciously. His concern was that it sometimes failed, leaving large numbers of people unemployed. In his analysis of the business cycle, Hayek identified that the major problem was the increase in the supply of money. Government intervention, through the central banks, drove interest rates down and made credit artificially cheap. Consequently, businesses received false signals from the credit market and made investment errors, particularly in relation to capital goods. Moreover, as the credit was not created by savings, the customers did not have the funds to purchase the resulting consumer goods. Then these malinvestments failed and a bust ensued.

During the 1930s, with general public approval, governments intervened in the social and economic life of their nations. There was a distrust for the market and disdain for individual decision-making. Hayek feared that empowering governments with increasing economic control would lead to the horrors of Nazi Germany and fascist Italy, rather than the desired utopia. In his best-known work, *The Road to Serfdom* (1944), Hayek meditates on the relationship between government authority and individual liberty. It is a passionate warning of the dangers of state control over the means of production.

Hayek's enduring legacy that centrally controlled economies are doomed to failure because they encroach unacceptably on personal liberty and that they are unable to allocate scarce resources efficiently were explained in *The Constitution of Liberty* (1960).

> Hayek's paper, *The Use of Knowledge in Society* is an important contribution to economic thought. It explains how individuals acquire and utilise knowledge through the market process. It provides the theoretical underpinning for the tale about the price miracle, told so well by Leonard Read in *I, Pencil*. It is a complex essay filled with abstract ideas, but the effort needed to understand it is worthwhile. Persevere. A complete understanding may require a second or third reading.

The use of knowledge in society

F.A. Hayek

What is the problem we wish to solve when we try to construct a rational economic order? On certain familiar assumptions the answer is simple enough. *If* we possess all the relevant information, *if* we can start out from a given system of preferences, and *if* we command complete knowledge of available means, the problem which remains is purely one of logic. That is, the answer to the question of what is the best use of the available means is implicit in our assumptions. The conditions which the solution of this optimum problem must satisfy have been fully worked out and can be stated best in mathematical form: put at their briefest, they are that the marginal rates of substitution between any two commodities or factors must be the same in all their different uses.

This, however, is emphatically *not* the economic problem which society faces. And the economic calculus which we have developed to solve this logical problem, though an important step toward the solution of the economic problem of society, does not yet provide an answer to it. The reason for this is that the "data" from which the economic calculus starts are never for the whole society "given" to a single mind which could work out the implications and can never be so given.

The peculiar character of the problem of a rational economic order is determined precisely by the fact that the knowledge of the circumstances of which we must make use never exists in concentrated or integrated form but solely as the dispersed bits of incomplete and frequently contradictory knowledge which all the separate individuals possess. The economic problem of society is thus not merely a problem of how to allocate "given" resources – if "given" is taken to mean given to a single mind which deliberately solves the problem set by these "data." It is rather a problem of how to secure the best use of resources known to any of the members of society, for ends whose relative importance only these individuals know. Or, to put it briefly, it is a problem of the utilization of knowledge which is not given to anyone in its totality.

This character of the fundamental problem has, I am afraid, been obscured rather than illuminated by many of the recent refinements of economic theory, particularly by many of the uses made of mathematics. Though the problem with which I want primarily to deal in this paper is the problem of a rational economic organization, I shall in its course be led again and again to point to its close connections with certain methodological questions. Many of the points I wish to make are indeed conclusions toward which diverse paths of reasoning have unexpectedly converged. But, as I now see these problems, this is no accident. It seems to me that many of the current disputes with regard to both economic theory and economic policy have their common origin in a misconception about the nature of the economic problem of society. This misconception in turn is due to an erroneous transfer to social phenomena of the habits of thought we have developed in dealing with the phenomena of nature.

In ordinary language, we describe by the word "planning" the complex of interrelated decisions about the allocation of our available resources. All economic activity is in this sense planning; and in any society in which many people collaborate, this planning, whoever does it, will in some measure have to be based on knowledge which, in the first instance, is not given to the planner but to somebody else, which somehow will have to be conveyed to the planner. The various ways in which the knowledge on which people base their plans is communicated to them is the crucial problem for any theory explaining the economic process, and the problem of what is the best way of utilizing knowledge initially dispersed among all the people is at least one of the main problems of economic policy – or of designing an efficient economic system.

The answer to this question is closely connected with that other question which arises here, that of *who* is to do the planning. It is about this question that all the dispute about "economic planning" centers. This is not a dispute about whether planning is to be done or not. It is a dispute as to whether planning is to be done centrally, by one authority for the whole economic system, or is to be divided among many individuals. Planning in the specific sense in which the term is used in contemporary controversy necessarily means central planning – direction of the whole economic system according to one unified plan. Competition, on the other hand, means decentralized planning by many separate persons. The halfway house between the two, about which many people talk but which few like when they see it, is the delegation of planning to organized industries, or, in other words, monopoly.

Which of these systems is likely to be more efficient depends mainly on the question under which of them we can expect that fuller use will be made of the existing knowledge. And this, in turn, depends on whether we are more likely to succeed in putting at the disposal of a single central authority all the knowledge which ought to be used but which is initially dispersed among many different individuals, or in conveying to the individuals such additional knowledge as they need in order to enable them to fit their plans with those of others.

It will at once be evident that on this point the position will be different with respect to different kinds of knowledge; and the answer to our question will therefore largely turn on the relative importance of the different kinds of knowledge; those more likely to be at the disposal of particular individuals and those which we should with greater confidence expect to find in the possession of an authority made up of suitably chosen experts. If it is today so widely assumed that the latter will be in a better position, this is because one kind of knowledge, namely, scientific knowledge, occupies now so prominent a place in public imagination that we tend to forget that it is not the only kind that is relevant. It may be admitted that, as far as scientific knowledge is concerned, a body of suitably chosen experts may be in the best position to command all the best knowledge available—though this is of course merely shifting the difficulty to the problem of selecting the experts. What I wish to point out is that, even assuming that this problem can be readily solved, it is only a small part of the wider problem.

Today it is almost heresy to suggest that scientific knowledge is not the sum of all knowledge. But a little reflection will show that there is beyond question a body of very important but unorganized knowledge which cannot possibly be called scientific in the sense of knowledge of general rules: the knowledge of the particular circumstances of time and place. It is with respect to this that practically every individual has some advantage over all others because he possesses unique information of which beneficial use might be made, but of which use can be made only if the decisions depending on it are left to him or are made with his active coöperation.

We need to remember only how much we have to learn in any occupation after we have completed our theoretical training, how big a part of our working life we spend learning particular jobs, and how valuable an asset in all walks of life is knowledge of people, of local conditions, and of special circumstances. To know of and put to use a machine not fully employed, or somebody's skill which could be better utilized, or to be aware of a surplus stock which can be drawn upon during an interruption of supplies, is socially quite as useful as the knowledge of better alternative techniques. And the shipper who earns his living from using otherwise empty or half-filled journeys of tramp-steamers, or the estate agent whose whole knowledge is almost exclusively one of temporary opportunities, or the *arbitrageur* who gains from local differences of commodity prices, are all performing eminently useful functions based on special knowledge of circumstances of the fleeting moment not known to others.

It is a curious fact that this sort of knowledge should today be generally regarded with a kind of contempt and that anyone who by such knowledge gains an advantage over somebody better equipped with theoretical or technical knowledge is thought to have acted almost disreputably. To gain an advantage from better knowledge of facilities of communication or transport is sometimes regarded as almost dishonest, although it is quite as important that society make use of the best opportunities in this respect as in using the latest scientific discoveries.

This prejudice has in a considerable measure affected the attitude toward commerce in general compared with that toward production. Even economists who regard themselves as definitely immune to the crude materialist fallacies of the past constantly commit the same mistake where activities directed toward the acquisition of such practical knowledge are concerned—apparently because in their scheme of things all such knowledge is supposed to be "given". The common idea now seems to be that all such knowledge should as a matter of course be readily at the command of everybody, and the reproach of irrationality levelled against the existing economic order is frequently based on the fact that it is not so available. This view disregards the fact that the method by which such knowledge can be made as widely available as possible is precisely the problem to which we have to find an answer.

If it is fashionable today to minimize the importance of the knowledge of the particular circumstances of time and place, this is closely connected with the smaller importance which is now attached to change as such. Indeed, there are few points on which the assumptions made (usually only implicitly) by the "planners" differ from those of their opponents as much as with regard to the significance and frequency of changes which will make substantial alterations of production plans necessary. Of course, if detailed economic plans could be laid down for fairly long periods in advance and then closely adhered to, so that no further economic decisions of importance would be required, the task of drawing up a comprehensive plan governing all economic activity would be much less formidable.

It is, perhaps, worth stressing that economic problems arise always and only in consequence of change. So long as things continue as before, or at least as they were expected to, there arise no new problems requiring a decision, no need to form a new plan. The belief that changes, or at least day-to-day adjustments, have become less important in modern times implies the contention that economic problems also have become less important. This belief in the decreasing importance of change is, for that reason, usually held by the same people who argue that the importance of economic considerations has been driven into the background by the growing importance of technological knowledge.

Is it true that, with the elaborate apparatus of modern production, economic decisions are required only at long intervals, as when a new factory is to be erected or a new process to be introduced? Is it true that, once a plant has been built, the rest is all more or less mechanical, determined by the character of the plant, and leaving little to be changed in adapting to the ever-changing circumstances of the moment?

The fairly widespread belief in the affirmative is not, as far as I can ascertain, borne out by the practical experience of the businessman. In a competitive industry at any rate—and such an industry alone can serve as a test—the task of keeping cost from rising requires constant struggle, absorbing a great part of the energy of the manager. How easy it is for an inefficient manager to dissipate the differentials on which profitability rests, and that it is possible, with the same technical facilities, to produce with a great variety of costs, are among the commonplaces of business experience which do not seem to be equally familiar in the study of the economist. The very strength of the desire, constantly voiced by producers and engineers, to be allowed to proceed untrammeled by considerations of money costs, is eloquent testimony to the extent to which these factors enter into their daily work.

One reason why economists are increasingly apt to forget about the constant small changes which make up the whole economic picture is probably their growing preoccupation with statistical aggregates, which show a very much greater stability than the movements of the detail. The comparative stability of the aggregates cannot, however, be accounted for—as the statisticians occasionally seem to be inclined to do—by the "law of large numbers" or the mutual compensation of random changes. The number of elements with which we have to deal is not large enough for such accidental forces to produce stability. The continuous flow of goods and services is maintained by constant deliberate adjustments, by new dispositions made every day in the light of circumstances not known the day before, by B stepping in at once when A fails to deliver. Even the large and highly mechanized plant keeps going largely because of an environment upon which it can draw for all sorts of unexpected needs; tiles for its roof, stationery for its forms, and all the thousand and one kinds of equipment in which it cannot be self-contained and which the plans for the operation of the plant require to be readily available in the market.

This is, perhaps, also the point where I should briefly mention the fact that the sort of knowledge with which I have been concerned is knowledge of the kind which by its nature cannot enter into statistics and therefore cannot be conveyed to any central authority in statistical form. The statistics which such a central authority would have to use would have to be arrived at precisely by abstracting from minor differences between the things, by lumping together, as resources of one kind, items which differ as regards location, quality, and other particulars, in a way which may be very significant for the specific decision. It follows from this that central planning based on statistical information by its nature cannot take direct account of these circumstances of time and place and that the central planner will have to find some way or other in which the decisions depending on them can be left to the "man on the spot."

If we can agree that the economic problem of society is mainly one of rapid adaptation to changes in the particular circumstances of time and place, it would seem to follow that the ultimate decisions must be left to the people who are familiar with these circumstances, who know directly of the relevant changes and of the resources immediately available to meet them.

We cannot expect that this problem will be solved by first communicating all this knowledge to a central board which, after integrating *all* knowledge, issues its orders. We must solve it by some form of decentralization. But this answers only part of our problem. We need decentralization because only thus can we ensure that the knowledge of the particular circumstances of time and place will be promptly used. But the "man on the spot" cannot decide solely on the basis of his limited but intimate knowledge of the facts of his immediate surroundings. There still remains the problem of communicating to him such further information as he needs to fit his decisions into the whole pattern of changes of the larger economic system.

How much knowledge does he need to do so successfully? Which of the events which happen beyond the horizon of his immediate knowledge are of relevance to his immediate decision, and how much of them need he know?

There is hardly anything that happens anywhere in the world that *might* not have an effect on the decision he ought to make. But he need not know of these events as such, nor of *all* their effects. It does not matter for him *why* at the particular moment more screws of one size than of another are wanted, *why* paper bags are more readily available than canvas bags, or *why* skilled labor, or particular machine tools, have for the moment become more difficult to obtain. All that is significant for him is *how much more or less* difficult to procure they have become compared with other things with which he is also concerned, or how much more or less urgently wanted are the alternative things he produces or uses. It is always a question of the relative importance of the particular things with which he is concerned, and the causes which alter their relative importance are of no interest to him beyond the effect on those concrete things of his own environment.

It is in this connection that what I have called the "economic calculus" proper helps us, at least by analogy, to see how this problem can be solved, and in fact is being solved, by the price system.

Even the single controlling mind, in possession of all the data for some small, self-contained economic system, would not—every time some small adjustment in the allocation of resources had to be made—go explicitly through all the relations between ends and means which might possibly be affected. It is indeed the great contribution of the pure logic of choice that it has demonstrated conclusively that even such a single mind could solve this kind of problem only by constructing and constantly using rates of equivalence (or "values," or "marginal rates of substitution"), *i.e.,* by attaching to each kind of scarce resource a numerical index which cannot be derived from any property possessed by that particular thing, but which reflects, or in which is condensed, its significance in view of the whole means-end structure. In any small change, he will have to consider only these quantitative indices (or "values") in which all the relevant information is concentrated; and, by adjusting the quantities one by one, he can appropriately rearrange his dispositions without having to solve the whole puzzle *ab initio* or without needing at any stage to survey it at once in all its ramifications.

Fundamentally, in a system in which the knowledge of the relevant facts is dispersed among many people, prices can act to coördinate the separate actions of different people in the same way as subjective values help the individual to coördinate the parts of his plan.

It is worth contemplating for a moment a very simple and commonplace instance of the action of the price system to see what precisely it accomplishes. Assume that somewhere in the world a new opportunity for the use of some raw material, say, tin, has arisen, or that one of the sources of supply of tin has been eliminated. It does not matter for our purpose—and it is very significant that it does not matter—which of these two causes has made tin more scarce. All that the users of tin need to know is that some of the tin they used to consume is now more profitably employed elsewhere and that, in consequence, they must economize tin. There is no need for the great majority of them even to know where the more urgent need has arisen, or in favor of what other needs they ought to husband the supply. If only some of them know directly of the new demand, and switch resources over to it, and if the people who are aware of the new gap thus created in turn fill it from still other sources, the effect will rapidly spread throughout the whole economic system and influence not only all the uses of tin but also those of its substitutes and the substitutes of these substitutes, the supply of all the things made of tin, and their substitutes, and so on; and all this without the great majority of those instrumental in bringing about these substitutions knowing anything at all about the original cause of these changes.

The whole acts as one market, not because any of its members survey the whole field, but because their limited individual fields of vision sufficiently overlap so that through many intermediaries the relevant information is communicated to all. The mere fact that there is one price for any commodity—or rather that local prices are connected in a manner determined by the cost of transport, etc.—brings about the solution which (it is just conceptually possible) might have been arrived at by one single mind possessing all the information which is in fact dispersed among all the people involved in the process.

We must look at the price system as such a mechanism for communicating information if we want to understand its real function—a function which, of course, it fulfils less perfectly as prices grow more rigid. (Even when quoted prices have become quite rigid, however, the forces which would operate through changes in price still operate to a considerable extent through changes in the other terms of the contract.) The most significant fact about this system is the economy of knowledge with which it operates, or how little the individual participants need to know in order to be able to take the right action. In abbreviated form, by a kind of symbol, only the most essential information is passed on and passed on only to those concerned. It is more than a metaphor to describe the price system as a kind of machinery for registering change, or a system of telecommunications which enables individual producers to watch merely the movement of a few pointers, as an engineer might watch the hands of a few dials, in order to adjust their activities to changes of which they may never know more than is reflected in the price movement.

Of course, these adjustments are probably never "perfect" in the sense in which the economist conceives of them in his equilibrium analysis. But I fear that our theoretical habits of approaching the problem with the assumption of more or less perfect knowledge on the part of almost everyone has made us somewhat blind to the true function of the price mechanism and led us to apply rather misleading standards in judging its efficiency. The marvel is that in a case like that of a scarcity of one raw material, without an order being issued, without more than perhaps a handful of people knowing the cause, tens of thousands of people whose identity could not be ascertained by months of investigation, are made to use the material or its products more sparingly; *i.e.,* they move in the right direction. This is enough of a marvel even if, in a constantly changing world, not all will hit it off so perfectly that their profit rates will always be maintained at the same constant or "normal" level.

I have deliberately used the word "marvel" to shock the reader out of the complacency with which we often take the working of this mechanism for granted. I am convinced that if it were the result of deliberate human design, and if the people guided by the price changes understood that their decisions have significance far beyond their immediate aim, this mechanism would have been acclaimed as one of the greatest triumphs of the human mind.

Its misfortune is the double one that it is not the product of human design and that the people guided by it usually do not know why they are made to do what they do. But those who clamour for "conscious direction"—and who cannot believe that anything which has evolved without design (and even without our understanding it) should solve problems which we should not be able to solve consciously—should remember this: The problem is precisely how to extend the span of our utilization of resources beyond the span of the control of any one mind; and therefore, how to dispense with the need of conscious control, and how to provide inducements which will make the individuals do the desirable things without anyone having to tell them what to do.

The problem which we meet here is by no means peculiar to economics but arises in connection with nearly all truly social phenomena, with language and with most of our cultural inheritance, and constitutes really the central theoretical problem of all social science. As Alfred Whitehead has said in another connection, "It is a profoundly erroneous truism, repeated by all copy-books and by eminent people when they are making speeches, that we should cultivate the habit of thinking what we are doing. The precise opposite is the case. Civilization advances by extending the number of important operations which we can perform without thinking about them."

This is of profound significance in the social field. We make constant use of formulas, symbols, and rules whose meaning we do not understand and through the use of which we avail ourselves of the assistance of knowledge which individually we do not possess. We have developed these practices and institutions by building upon habits and institutions which have proved successful in their own sphere and which have in turn become the foundation of the civilization we have built up.

The price system is just one of those formations which man has learned to use (though he is still very far from having learned to make the best use of it) after he had stumbled upon it without understanding it. Through it not only a division of labor but also a coördinated utilization of resources based on an equally divided knowledge has become possible.

The people who like to deride any suggestion that this may be so usually distort the argument by insinuating that it asserts that by some miracle just that sort of system has spontaneously grown up which is best suited to modern civilization. It is the other way round: man has been able to develop that division of labor on which our civilization is based because he happened to stumble upon a method which made it possible. Had he not done so, he might still have developed some other, altogether different, type of civilization, something like the "state" of the termite ants, or some other altogether unimaginable type. All that we can say is that nobody has yet succeeded in designing an alternative system in which certain features of the existing one can be preserved which are dear even to those who most violently assail it—such as particularly the extent to which the individual can choose his pursuits and consequently freely use his own knowledge and skill.

It is in many ways fortunate that the dispute about the indispensability of the price system for any rational calculation in a complex society is now no longer conducted entirely between camps holding different political views. The thesis that without the price system we could not preserve a society based on such extensive division of labor as ours was greeted with a howl of derision when it was first advanced by von Mises twenty-five years ago. Today the difficulties which some still find in accepting it are no longer mainly political, and this makes for an atmosphere much more conducive to reasonable discussion. When we find Leon Trotsky arguing that "economic accounting is unthinkable without market relations"; when Professor Oscar Lange promises Professor von Mises a statue in the marble halls of the future Central Planning Board; and when Professor Abba P. Lerner rediscovers Adam Smith and emphasizes that the essential utility of the price system consists in inducing the individual, while seeking his own interest, to do what is in the general interest, the differences can indeed no longer be ascribed to political prejudice. The remaining dissent seems clearly to be due to purely intellectual, and more particularly methodological, differences.

A recent statement by Professor Joseph Schumpeter in his *Capitalism, Socialism, and Democracy* provides a clear illustration of one of the methodological differences which I have in mind. Its author is pre-eminent among those economists who approach economic phenomena in the light of a certain branch of positivism. To him these phenomena accordingly appear as objectively given quantities of commodities impinging directly upon each other, almost, it would seem, without any intervention of human minds. Only against this background can I account for the following (to me startling) pronouncement. Professor Schumpeter argues that the possibility of a rational calculation in the absence of markets for the factors of production follows for the theorist "from the elementary proposition that consumers in evaluating ('demanding') consumers' goods *ipso facto* also evaluate the means of production which enter into the production of these goods."

Taken literally, this statement is simply untrue. The consumers do nothing of the kind. What Professor Schumpeter's *"ipso facto"* presumably means is that the valuation of the factors of production is implied in, or follows necessarily from, the valuation of consumers' goods. But this, too, is not correct. Implication is a logical relationship which can be meaningfully asserted only of propositions simultaneously present to one and the same mind. It is evident, however, that the values of the factors of production do not depend solely on the valuation of the consumers' goods but also on the conditions of supply of the various factors of production. Only to a mind to which all these facts were simultaneously known would the answer necessarily follow from the facts given to it. The practical problem, however, arises precisely because these facts are never so given to a single mind, and because, in consequence, it is necessary that in the solution of the problem knowledge should be used that is dispersed among many people.

The problem is thus in no way solved if we can show that all the facts, *if* they were known to a single mind (as we hypothetically assume them to be given to the observing economist), would uniquely determine the solution; instead we must show how a solution is produced by the interactions of people each of whom possesses only partial knowledge. To assume all the knowledge to be given to a single mind in the same manner in which we assume it to be given to us as the explaining economists is to assume the problem away and to disregard everything that is important and significant in the real world.

That an economist of Professor Schumpeter's standing should thus have fallen into a trap which the ambiguity of the term "datum" sets to the unwary can hardly be explained as a simple error. It suggests rather that there is something fundamentally wrong with an approach which habitually disregards an essential part of the phenomena with which we have to deal: the unavoidable imperfection of man's knowledge and the consequent need for a process by which knowledge is constantly communicated and acquired. Any approach, such as that of much of mathematical economics with its simultaneous equations, which in effect starts from the assumption that people's *knowledge* corresponds with the objective *facts* of the situation, systematically leaves out what is our main task to explain. I am far from denying that in our system equilibrium analysis has a useful function to perform. But when it comes to the point where it misleads some of our leading thinkers into believing that the situation which it describes has direct relevance to the solution of practical problems, it is high time that we remember that it does not deal with the social process at all and that it is no more than a useful preliminary to the study of the main problem.

The Use of Knowledge in Society was first published in *The American Economic Review*, vol. 35, no. 4, 1945, p. 519–30. Permission to reprint was granted by The American Economic Association.

4

Capitalism made the
customer king

The erudite Yuval Noah Harari's *Sapiens: A History of Humankind* (2014) is a wonderful story filled with information and insights. However, some of it may be incorrect. At one point, Mr Harari proposes that life was better for humans prior to the agricultural revolution. That was when you could forage for figs and nuts in the morning, occasionally do a little hunting, and then sit around socialising in the afternoon and evening. It sounds pleasant enough if you ignore the simultaneous threats of the sabre tooth tiger and the guys from the neighbouring tribe who desire your womenfolk. There was much more violence, including domestic violence, in the tribal hunter–gatherer era than Mr Harari let on.

A couple of years ago, I sat in my comfortable Sigurd Ressell chair reading *Sapiens* and generally enjoying the benefits of twenty-first-century life. The sun was streaming in through the three-metre-high steel-and-glass window. In the background, using my favourite music streaming service, I listened to Louis Armstrong's 'What a wonderful world'. Idyllic. It was then that I knew that Mr Harari was wrong.

In Australia, we live in one of the most free and prosperous societies in the history of humankind. Why should we be so lucky? Two suggestions: democracy and capitalism.

In the political sphere, democracy has provided citizens with sovereignty, with government by the people. We usually credit John Locke for this idea. Locke influenced the Glorious Revolution in Britain in 1688. The people invited William of Orange to be king, but under strict conditions: that he be subject to the will of the parliament. In fact, the ideas for this had been bubbling away in England for centuries. They had come to a head on previous occasions, including the passing of Magna Carta in 1215 and the Peasants' Revolt led by Wat Tyler in 1381. But John Locke was the one who articulated the idea of democracy for his own and future generations. [25]

One hundred years later, Locke's philosophies influenced Thomas Jefferson and his colleagues when they wrote the United States Declaration of Independence.

> *We hold these truths to be self-evident,*
> *That all men are created equal,*
> *That they are endowed by their creator*
> *with certain unalienable Rights,*
> *That among these are Life, Liberty and*
> *the Pursuit of Happiness.*
> *That to secure these rights,*
> *Governments are instituted among Men,*
> *Deriving their just powers from the consent of the governed.*

In Australia, as in the United States, we are free to influence the laws under which we live. Every few years we can vote to choose which politicians and political parties may represent us in parliament. We vote for those we hope will best represent our views and our interests. This system is not fine-grained enough to be perfect, but it is better than being subject to the arbitrary decisions of an authoritarian ruler.

In a similar way, free markets provide citizens with sovereignty over which goods and services are produced. Prior to the industrial revolution, artisans made objects for aristocrats. Capitalism brought not simply mass production, but mass production to satisfy the needs of the masses. The workers became the buyers of their own product. They became customers.

---

25   Hannan (2013)

Nowadays, we vote every time we purchase, or refrain from purchasing, a good or service. We vote every time we do the weekly shopping and determine which brand of cereal to purchase or which fruits and vegetables to select. We vote when we choose to cook spaghetti at home rather than eat at the local Italian restaurant. We vote when we choose new clothes. We vote when we choose who will be our doctor or dentist. We vote when we choose which football team to barrack for. We vote on long-term purchases when we decide it is time for a new car. Sometimes our votes are not even direct comparisons; we may choose a family holiday and defer the purchase of the new car.

We vote every time we swap one supplier for another. Perhaps we have always driven BMW, but this time we choose Mercedes. Perhaps we used to shop for groceries at Woolworths and now change to a Coles. Perhaps we used to buy shirts from Henry Bucks shop on Collins Street, but now buy online from Charles Tyrwhitt.

In this way, as consumers we are making the decisions on what to buy and where, and therefore what is produced and where it is sold. Economic power, in a market economy, is in the hands of the consumers. Capitalism might be more accurately called 'economic democracy'.

In his 1955 classic, *The Practice of Management,* Peter Drucker wrote that "the purpose of a business is to create customers". [26] It is a wonderful insight. A free market economy is never still; it is always changing and improving. It is forever encouraging enterprising people to exert themselves in the interest of others, to create new products or better ways to package them or better ways to deliver them to the market. In a free market economy, the customer is always right. As entrepreneurs innovate and take risks, interpreting what the customer wants, they create prosperity. They succeed by providing value for their customers.

The customers are sovereign. They are the fortunate ones who benefit from the ingenuity of the entrepreneurs.

---

26   Drucker (1968), p. 52

Ludwig von Mises (1891–1973)

Ludwig von Mises was one of the intellectual giants of the twentieth century. His contributions to economics, political theory and the social sciences were profound.

Born in Lemberg[27] in the Austro-Hungarian empire in 1881, Mises graduated from the University of Vienna with a Doctor of Laws in 1906. From 1909, he worked in economic public policy for the Austrian Chamber of Commerce, combining this with research, writing scholarly works and lecturing at the university.

In the 1920s, Mises ran a fortnightly *privatseminar* for a select group of young Viennese intellectuals, many of whom later became famous in their own right. They included economists Gottfried von Haberler, Friedrich Hayek, Fritz Machlup, Oskar Morgenstern, Richard von Strigl and Paul Rosenstein-Rodan, plus philosopher Felix Kaufmann, sociologist Alfred Shutz and philosopher of history Erich Voegelin.

During this period Mises wrote his path-breaking work on monetary theory, *The Theory of Money and Credit* (1912). His other works included *Socialism* (1922), *Liberalism* (1927), *A Critique of Interventionism* (1929) and *Epistemological Problems of Economics* (1933).

27　This was the German name for the city of Lviv in Ukraine.

In 1934, after forty years in Vienna, concerned about the apparent inevitability of a Nazi takeover, Mises accepted a position at the Graduate Institute of International Studies in Geneva, Switzerland. There, he was able to devote himself completely to his study of economics, which resulted in *Nationalokonomie*, the basis for his magnum opus, *Human Action: A Treatise on Economics* In 1940, blacklisted by the Nazis and feeling unsafe, Mises and his wife, Margit, escaped to the United States.

Mises arrived in New York, aged nearly 60, with no job and not completely fluent in English. The first few years were not easy. A grant from the Rockefeller Foundation to the National Bureau of Economic Research provided him with a modest livelihood. With support from Henry Hazlitt, Mises undertook a several assignments for the National Association of Manufacturers. He gave guest lectures at Columbia, Harvard and Princeton universities. Two books, *Omnipotent Government* and *Bureaucracy*, were published by Yale University Press in 1944. By 1946 Mises held a visiting professorship at New York University's Graduate School of Business Administration and a staff position at Leonard Read's Foundation for Economic Education.

Mises spent his whole life at odds with the prevailing views of the economics profession. He challenged the German Historical School, which provided the economic ideas for socialism, and Keynes, whose interventionist ideas provided the intellectual underpinning for the New Deal, and the movement to mathematical economics and econometrics.

In 1949, Mises published *Human Action: A Treatise on Economics*, in English. It is a comprehensive treatise on economics. In it he developed universal laws of economics, integrating the elements of economic theory that had been his life's work. *Human Action* is a masterpiece. It sets economics within a more universal science of praxeology – the pure logic of choice.

Mises posited that our knowledge of praxeology was a priori: 'the only way to a cognition of these theorems is logical analysis or our inherent knowledge of the category of action'.[28] He believed that people have

---

28   Mises (1949), p. 64

purposes, and they try to achieve their goals. They act because they want to change things for the better, to eliminate some felt dissatisfaction. Action is the use of means to achieve ends, and people choose their most highly valued preferences. All action is rational in that it is attempting to use a means to achieve an end. (That does not preclude people from making mistakes.)

Mises's theories apply to all peoples and all times. His contributions are vast. Some of the more significant include that prices are determined by subjective values; economic calculation requires the price mechanism to determine the most economic use of resources; socialism cannot allocate resources efficiently because it lacks this price mechanism; social cooperation through the free market makes possible the division of labour; trade and specialisation are keys to continued prosperity; the role of the entrepreneur is crucial – not only to correct disequilibria in the market place but also to discover opportunities; government manipulation of the money supply and interest rates causes recessions; and that humans gain more from peaceful exchange than from destructive struggles.

Mises continued to write prolifically and was still presenting seminars at the age of 90. Now, years after his death, there is a resurgence of Austrian economics. His contributions are being recognised and his ideas widely understood.

The Ludwig von Mises Institute, founded in 1982 with the collaboration of Margit von Mises, is a thriving research and educational centre for classical liberalism, libertarian political theory and the Austrian school of economics. It provides onsite and online courses, scholarships, educational materials, conferences, media and literature.

> In his lecture, *Liberty & Property*, which was presented at the opening session of the ninth meeting of The Mont Pelerin Society, held in Princeton, New Jersey, on 8 September 1958, Mises identifies the crucial difference that capitalism made. It shifted the locus of control of economic activity from the elites to the common person. The customer became king.

Liberty & Property

Ludwig von Mises

1.

At the end of the eighteenth century there prevailed two notions of liberty, each of them very different from what we have in mind today referring to liberty and freedom. The first of these conceptions was purely academic and without any application to the conduct of political affairs. It was an idea derived from the books of the ancient authors, the study of which was then the sum and substance of higher education. In the eyes of these Greek and Roman writers, freedom was not something that had to be granted to all men. It was a privilege of the minority, to be withheld from the majority. What the Greeks called democracy was, in the light of present-day terminology, not what Lincoln called government by the people, but oligarchy, the sovereignty of full-right citizens in a community in which the masses were meteques or slaves. Even this rather limited freedom after the fourth century before Christ was not dealt with by the philosophers, historians, and orators as a practical constitutional institution. As they saw it, it was a feature of the past irretrievably lost. They bemoaned the passing of this golden age, but they did not know any method of returning to it.

The second notion of liberty was no less oligarchic, although it was not inspired by any literary reminiscences. It was the ambition of the landed aristocracy, and sometimes also of urban patricians, to preserve their privileges against the rising power of royal absolutism. In most parts of continental Europe, the princes remained victorious in these conflicts. Only in England and in the Netherlands did the gentry and the urban patricians succeed in defeating the dynasties. But what they won was not freedom for all, but only freedom for an elite, for a minority of the people.

We must not condemn as hypocrites the men who in those ages praised liberty, while they preserved the legal disabilities of the many, even serfdom and slavery. They were faced with a problem which they did not know how to solve satisfactorily. The traditional system of production was too narrow for a continually rising population. The number of people for whom there was, in a full sense of the term, no room left by the pre-capitalistic methods of agriculture, and artisanship was increasing. These supernumeraries were starving paupers. They were a menace to the preservation of the existing order of society and, for a long time, nobody could think of another order, a state of affairs, that would feed all of these poor wretches. There could not be any question of granting them full civil rights, still less of giving them a share of the conduct of affairs of state. The only expedient the rulers knew was to keep them quiet by resorting to force.

2.

The pre-capitalistic system of production was restrictive. Its historical basis was military conquest. The victorious kings had given the land to their paladins. These aristocrats were lords in the literal meaning of the word, as they did not depend on the patronage of consumers buying or abstaining from buying on a market. On the other hand, they themselves were the main customers of the processing industries which, under the guild system, were organized on a corporative scheme. This scheme was opposed to innovation. It forbade deviation from the traditional methods of production. The number of people for whom there were jobs even in agriculture or in the arts and crafts was limited. Under these conditions, many a man, to use the words of Malthus, had to discover that "at nature's mighty feast there is no vacant cover for him" and that "she tells him to be gone." But some of these outcasts nevertheless managed to survive, begot children, and made the number of destitute grow hopelessly more and more.

But then came capitalism. It is customary to see the radical innovations that capitalism brought about in the substitution of the mechanical factory for the more primitive and less efficient methods of the artisans' shops. This is a rather superficial view. The characteristic feature of capitalism that distinguishes it from pre-capitalist methods of production was its new principle of marketing. Capitalism is not simply mass production, but mass production to satisfy the needs of the masses. The arts and crafts of the good old days had catered almost exclusively to the wants of the well-to-do. But the factories produced cheap goods for the many. All the early factories turned out was designed to serve the masses, the same strata that worked in the factories. They served them either by supplying them directly or indirectly by exporting and thus providing for them foreign food and raw materials. This principle of marketing was the signature of early capitalism as it is of present-day capitalism. The employees themselves are the customers consuming the much greater part of all goods produced. They are the sovereign customers who are "always right." Their buying or abstention from buying determines what has to be produced, in what quantity, and of what quality. In buying what suits them best they make some enterprises profit and expand and make other enterprises lose money and shrink. Thereby they are continually shifting control of the factors of production into the hands of those businessmen who are most successful in filling their wants. Under capitalism private property of the factors of production is a social function. The entrepreneurs, capitalists, and landowners are mandataries, as it were, of the consumers, and their mandate is revocable.

In order to be rich, it is not sufficient to have once saved and accumulated capital. It is necessary to invest it again and again in those lines in which it best fills the wants of the consumers. The market process is a daily repeated plebiscite, and it ejects inevitably from the ranks of profitable people those who do not employ their property according to the orders given by the public.

But business, the target of fanatical hatred on the part of all contemporary governments and self-styled intellectuals, acquires and preserves bigness only because it works for the masses. The plants that cater to the luxuries of the few never attain big size. The shortcoming of nineteenth-century historians and politicians was that they failed to realize that the workers were the main consumers of the products of industry. In their view, the wage earner was a man toiling for the sole benefit of a parasitic leisure class. They labored under the delusion that the factories had impaired the lot of the manual workers. If they had paid any attention to statistics they would easily have discovered the fallaciousness of their opinion. Infant mortality dropped, the average length of life was prolonged, the population multiplied, and the average common man enjoyed amenities of which even the well-to-do of earlier ages did not dream.

However this unprecedented enrichment of the masses was merely a by-product of the Industrial Revolution. Its main achievement was the transfer of economic supremacy from the owners of land to the totality of the population. The common man was no longer a drudge who had to be satisfied with the crumbs that fell from the tables of the rich.

The three pariah castes which were characteristic of the pre-capitalistic ages—the slaves, the serfs, and those people whom patristic and scholastic authors as well as British legislation from the sixteenth to the nineteenth centuries referred to as the poor—disappeared. Their scions became, in this new setting of business, not only free workers, but also customers.

This radical change was reflected in the emphasis laid by business on markets. What business needs first of all is markets and again markets. This was the watch-word of capitalistic enterprise. Markets, that means patrons, buyers, consumers. There is under capitalism one way to wealth: to serve the consumers better and cheaper than other people do.

Within the shop and factory the owner - or in the corporations, the representative of the shareholders, the president - is the boss. But this mastership is merely apparent and conditional. It is subject to the supremacy of the consumers. The consumer is king, is the real boss, and the manufacturer is done for if he does not outstrip his competitors in best serving consumers.

It was this great economic transformation that changed the face of the world. It very soon transferred political power from the hands of a privileged minority into the hands of the people. Adult franchise followed in the wake of industrial enfranchisement. The common man, to whom the market process had given the power to choose the entrepreneur and capitalists, acquired the analogous power in the field of government. He became a voter.

It has been observed by eminent economists, I think first by the late Frank A. Fetter, that the market is a democracy in which every penny gives a right to vote. It would be more correct to say that representative government by the people is an attempt to arrange constitutional affairs according to the model of the market, but this design can never be fully achieved. In the political field it is always the will of the majority that prevails, and the minorities must yield to it. It serves also minorities, provided they are not so insignificant in number as to become negligible.

The garment industry produces clothes not only for normal people, but also for the stout, and the publishing trade publishes not only westerns and detective stories for the crowd, but also books for discriminating readers. There is a second important difference. In the political sphere, there is no means for an individual or a small group of individuals to disobey the will of the majority. But in the intellectual field private property makes rebellion possible. The rebel has to pay a price for his independence; there are in this universe no prizes that can be won without sacrifices. But if a man is willing to pay the price, he is free to deviate from the ruling orthodoxy or neo-orthodoxy. What would conditions have been in the socialist commonwealth for heretics like Kierkegaard, Schopenhauer, Veblen, or Freud? For Monet, Courbet, Walt Whitman, Rilke, or Kafka?

In all ages, pioneers of new ways of thinking and acting could work only because private property made contempt of the majority's ways possible. Only a few of these separatists were themselves economically independent enough to defy the government into the opinions of the majority. But they found in the climate of the free economy among the public people prepared to aid and support them. What would Marx have done without his patron, the manufacturer Friedrich Engels?

3.

What vitiates entirely the socialists' economic critique of capitalism is their failure to grasp the sovereignty of the consumers in the market economy. They see only hierarchical organization of the various enterprises and plans, and are at a loss to realize that the profit system forces business to serve the consumers. In their dealings with their employers, the unions proceed as if only malice and greed were to prevent what they call management from paying higher wage rates. Their shortsightedness does not see anything beyond the doors of the factory. They and their henchmen talk about the concentration of economic power, and do not realize that economic power is ultimately vested in the hands of the buying public of which the employees themselves form the immense majority. Their inability to comprehend things as they are is reflected in such inappropriate metaphors as industrial kingdom and dukedoms. They are too dull to see the difference between a sovereign king or duke who could be dispossessed only by a more powerful conqueror and a "chocolate king" who forfeits his "kingdom" as soon as the customers prefer to patronize another supplier.

This distortion is at the bottom of all socialist plans. If any of the socialist chiefs had tried to earn his living by selling hot dogs, he would have learned something about the sovereignty of the customers. But they were professional revolutionaries, and their only job was to kindle civil war. Lenin's ideal was to build a nation's production effort according to the model of the post office, an outfit that does not depend on the consumers, because its deficits are covered by compulsory collection of taxes. "The whole of society," he said, was to "become one office and one factory."

He did not see that the very character of the office and the factory is entirely changed when it is alone in the world and no longer grants to people the opportunity to choose among the products and services of various enterprises. Because his blindness made it impossible for him to see the role the market and the consumers play under capitalism, he could not see the difference between freedom and slavery. Because in his eyes the workers were only workers and not also customers, he believed they were already slaves under capitalism, and that one did not change their status when nationalizing all plants and shops.

Socialism substitutes the sovereignty of a dictator, or committee of dictators, for the sovereignty of the consumers. Along with the economic sovereignty of the citizens disappears also their political sovereignty. To the unique production plan that annuls any planning on the part of the consumers corresponds in the constitutional sphere the one-party principle that deprives the citizens of any opportunity to plan the course of public affairs. Freedom is indivisible. He who has not the faculty to choose among various brands of canned food or soap, is also deprived of the power to choose between various political parties and programs and to elect the officeholders. He is no longer a man; he becomes a pawn in the hands of the supreme social engineer. Even his freedom to rear progeny will be taken away by eugenics.

Of course, the socialist leaders occasionally assure us that dictatorial tyranny is to last only for the period of transition from capitalism and representative government to the socialist millennium in which everybody's wants and wishes will be fully satisfied. Once the socialist regime is "sufficiently secure to risk criticism," Miss Joan Robinson, the eminent representative of the British neo-Cambridge school, is kind enough to promise us, "even independent philharmonic societies" will be allowed to exist.

Thus the liquidation of all dissenters is the condition that will bring us what the communists call freedom. From this point of view we may also understand what another distinguished Englishman, Mr. J.G. Crowther, had in mind when he praised inquisition as "beneficial to science when it protects a rising class." The meaning of all this is clear. When all people meekly bow to a dictator, there will no longer be any dissenters left for liquidation. Caligula, Torquemada, Robespierre would have agreed with this solution.

The socialists have engineered a semantic revolution in converting the meaning of terms into their opposite. In the vocabulary of their "Newspeak," as George Orwell called it, there is a term "the one-party principle." Now etymologically party is derived from the noun part. The brotherless part is no longer different from its antonym, the whole; it is identical with it. A brotherless party is not a party, and the one-party principle is in fact a no-party principle. It is a suppression of any kind of opposition. Freedom implies the right to choose between assent and dissent. But in Newspeak it means the duty to assent unconditionally and strict interdiction of dissent.

This reversal of the traditional connotation of all words of the political terminology is not merely a peculiarity of the language of the Russian Communists and their Fascist and Nazi disciples. The social order that in abolishing private property deprives the consumers of their autonomy and independence, and thereby subjects every man to the arbitrary discretion of the central planning board, could not win the support of the masses if they were not to camouflage its main character. The socialists would have never duped the voters if they had openly told them that their ultimate end is to cast them into bondage. For exoteric use they were forced to pay lip-service to the traditional appreciation of liberty.

4.

It was different in the esoteric discussions among the inner circles of the great conspiracy. There the initiated did not dissemble their intentions concerning liberty. Liberty was, in their opinion, certainly a good feature in the past in the frame of bourgeois society because it provided them with the opportunity to embark on their schemes. But once socialism has triumphed, there is no longer any need for free thought and autonomous action on the part of individuals. Any further change can only be a deviation from the perfect state that mankind has attained in reaching the bliss of socialism. Under such conditions, it would be simply lunacy to tolerate dissent.

Liberty, says the Bolshevist, is a bourgeois prejudice. The common man does not have any ideas of his own, he does not write books, does not hatch heresies, and does not invent new methods of production. He just wants to enjoy life. He has no use for the class interests of the intellectuals who make a living as professional dissenters and innovators.

This is certainly the most arrogant disdain of the plain citizen ever devised. There is no need to argue this point. For the question is not whether or not the common man can himself take advantage of the liberty to think, to speak, and to write books. The question is whether or not the sluggish routinist profits from the freedom granted to those who eclipse him in intelligence and will power. The common man may look with indifference and even contempt upon the dealings of better people. But he is delighted to enjoy all the benefits which the endeavors of the innovators put at his disposal. He has no comprehension of what in his eyes is merely inane hair-splitting. But as soon as these thoughts and theories are utilized by enterprising businessmen for satisfying some of his latent wishes, he hurries to acquire the new products. The common man is without doubt the main beneficiary of all the accomplishments of modern science and technology.

It is true, a man of average intellectual abilities has no chance to rise to the rank of a captain of industry. But the sovereignty that the market assigns to him in economic affairs stimulates technologists and promoters to convert to his use all the achievements of scientific research. Only people whose intellectual horizon does not extend beyond the internal organization of the factory and who do not realize what makes the businessmen run, fail to notice this fact.

The admirers of the Soviet system tell us again and again that freedom is not the supreme good. It is "not worth having," if it implies poverty. To sacrifice it in order to attain wealth for the masses, is in their eyes fully justified. But for a few unruly individualists who cannot adjust themselves to the ways of regular fellows, all people in Russia are perfectly happy. We may leave it undecided whether this happiness was also shared by the millions of Ukrainian peasants who died from starvation, by the inmates of the forced labor camps, and by the Marxian leaders who were purged. But we cannot pass over the fact that the standard of living was incomparably higher in the free countries of the West than in the communist East. In giving away liberty as the price to be paid for the acquisition of prosperity, the Russians made a poor bargain. They now have neither the one nor the other.

5.

Romantic philosophy labored under the illusion that in the early ages of history the individual was free and that the course of historical evolution deprived him of his primordial liberty. As Jean Jacques Rousseau saw it, nature accorded men freedom and society enslaved him. In fact, primeval man was at the mercy of every fellow who was stronger and therefore could snatch away from him the scarce means of subsistence. There is in nature nothing to which the name of liberty could be given. The concept of freedom always refers to social relations between men. True, society cannot realize the illusory concept of the individual's absolute independence. Within society everyone depends on what other people are prepared to contribute to his well-being in return for his own contribution to their well-being. Society is essentially the mutual exchange of services. As far as individuals have the opportunity to choose, they are free; if they are forced by violence or threat of violence to surrender to the terms of an exchange, no matter how they feel about it, they lack freedom. This slave is unfree precisely because the master assigns him his tasks and determines what he has to receive if he fulfills it.

As regards the social apparatus of repression and coercion, the government, there cannot be any question of freedom. Government is essentially the negation of liberty. It is the recourse to violence or threat of violence in order to make all people obey the orders of the government, whether they like it or not. As far as the government's jurisdiction extends, there is coercion, not freedom. Government is a necessary institution, the means to make the social system of cooperation work smoothly without being disturbed by violent acts on the part of gangsters whether of domestic or of foreign origin. Government is not, as some people like to say, a necessary evil; it is not an evil, but a means, the only means available to make peaceful human coexistence possible. But it is the opposite of liberty. It is beating, imprisoning, hanging.

Whatever a government does it is ultimately supported by the actions of armed constables. If the government operates a school or a hospital, the funds required are collected by taxes, i.e., by payments exacted from the citizens.

If we take into account the fact that, as human nature is, there can neither be civilization nor peace without the functioning of the government apparatus of violent action, we may call government the most beneficial human institution. But the fact remains that government is repression not freedom. Freedom is to be found only in the sphere in which government does not interfere. Liberty is always freedom from the government. It is the restriction of the government's interference. It prevails only in the fields in which the citizens have the opportunity to choose the way in which they want to proceed. Civil rights are the statutes that precisely circumscribe the sphere in which the men conducting the affairs of state are permitted to restrict the individuals' freedom to act.

The ultimate end that men aim at by establishing government is to make possible the operation of a definite system of social cooperation under the principle of the division of labor. If the social system which people want to have is socialism (communism, planning) there is no sphere of freedom left. All citizens are in every regard subject to orders of the government. The state is a total state; the regime is totalitarian. The government alone plans and forces everybody to behave according with this unique plan. In the market economy the individuals are free to choose the way in which they want to integrate themselves into the frame of social cooperation. As far as the sphere of market exchange extends, there is spontaneous action on the part of individuals. Under this system that is called laissez-faire, and which Ferdinand Lassalle dubbed as the nightwatchman state, there is freedom because there is a field in which individuals are free to plan for themselves.

The socialists must admit there cannot be any freedom under a socialist system. But they try to obliterate the difference between the servile state and economic freedom by denying that there is any freedom in the mutual exchange of commodities and services on the market. Every market exchange is, in the words of a school of pro-socialist lawyers, "a coercion over other people's liberty." There is, in their eyes, no difference worth mentioning between a man's paying a tax or a fine imposed by a magistrate, or his buying a newspaper or admission to a movie. In each of these cases the man is subject to governing power. He's not free, for, as Professor Hale says, a man's freedom means "the absence of any obstacle to his use of material goods." This means: I am not free, because a woman who has knitted a sweater, perhaps as a birthday present for her husband, puts an obstacle to my using it. I myself am restricting all other people's freedom because I object to their using my toothbrush. In doing this I am, according to this doctrine, exercising private governing power, which is analogous to public government power, the powers that the government exercises in imprisoning a man in Sing Sing.

Those expounding this amazing doctrine consistently conclude that liberty is nowhere to be found. They assert that what they call economic pressures do not essentially differ from the pressures the masters practice with regard to their slaves. They reject what they call private governmental power, but they don't object to the restriction of liberty by public government power. They want to concentrate all what they call restrictions of liberty in the hands of the government. They attack the institution of private property and the laws that, as they say, stand "ready to enforce property rights—that is, to deny liberty to anyone to act in a way which violates them."

A generation ago all housewives prepared soup by proceeding in accordance with the recipes that they had got from their mothers or from a cookbook. Today many housewives prefer to buy a canned soup, to warm it and to serve it to their family. But, say our learned doctors, the canning corporation is in a position to restrict the housewife's freedom because, in asking a price for the tin can, it puts an obstacle to her use of it. People who did not enjoy the privilege of being tutored by these eminent teachers, would say that the canned product was turned out by the cannery, and that the corporation in producing it removed the greatest obstacle to a consumer's getting and using a can, viz., its nonexistence. The mere essence of a product cannot gratify anybody without its existence. But they are wrong, say the doctors. The corporation dominates the housewife, it destroys by its excessive concentrated power over her individual freedom, and it is the duty of the government to prevent such a gross offense. Corporations, say, under the auspices of the Ford Foundation, another of this group, Professor Berle, must be subjected to the control of the government.

Why does our housewife buy the canned product rather than cling to the methods of her mother and grandmother? No doubt because she thinks this way of acting is more advantageous for her than the traditional custom. Nobody forced her. There were people—they are called jobbers, promoters, capitalists, speculators, stock exchange gamblers—who had the idea of satisfying a latent wish of millions of housewives by investing in the cannery industry. And there are other equally selfish capitalists who, in many hundreds of other corporations, provide consumers with many hundreds of other things. The better a corporation serves the public, the more customers it gets, the bigger it grows. Go into the home of the average American family and you will see for whom the wheels of the machines are turning.

In a free country nobody is prevented from acquiring riches by serving the consumers better than they are served already. What he needs is only brains and hard work. "Modern civilization, nearly all civilization," said Edwin Cannan, the last in a long line of eminent British economists, "is based on the principle of making things pleasant for those who please the market, and unpleasant for those who fail to do so." All this talk about the concentration of economic power is vain. The bigger a corporation is, the more people it serves, the more does it depend on pleasing the consumers, the many, the masses. Economic power, in the market economy, is in the hands of the consumers.

Capitalistic business is not perseverance in the once attained state of production. It is rather ceaseless innovation, daily repeated attempts to improve the provision of the consumers by new, better and cheaper products. Any actual state of production activities is merely transitory. There prevails incessantly the tendency to supplant what is already achieved by something that serves the consumers better. There is consequently under capitalism a continuous circulation of elites.

What characterizes the men whom one calls the captains of industry is the ability to contribute new ideas and to put them to work. However big a corporation must be, it is doomed as soon as it does not succeed in adjusting itself daily anew to the best possible methods of serving the consumers. But the politicians and other would-be reformers see only the structure of industry as it exists today. They think that they are cleaver enough to snatch from business control of the plants as they are today, and to manage them by sticking to already established routines. While the ambitious newcomer, who will be the tycoon of tomorrow, is already preparing plans for things unheard of before, all they have in mind is to conduct affairs along tracks already beaten.

There is no record of an industrial innovation contrived and put into practice by bureaucrats. If one does not want to plunge into stagnation, a free hand must be left to those today unknown men who have the ingenuity to lead mankind forward on the way to more and more satisfactory conditions. This is the main problem of a nation's economic organization.

Private property of the material factors of production is not a restriction of the freedom of all other people to choose what suits them best. It is, on the contrary, the means that assigns to the common man, in his capacity as a buyer, supremacy in all economic affairs. It is the means to stimulate a nation's most enterprising men to exert themselves to the best of their abilities in the service of all of the people.

6.

However, one does not exhaustively describe the sweeping changes that capitalism brought about in the conditions of the common man if one merely deals with the supremacy he enjoys on the market as a consumer and in the affairs of state as a voter and with the unprecedented improvement of his standard of living. No less important is the fact that capitalism has made it possible for him to save, to accumulate capital and to invest it.

The gulf that in the pre-capitalistic status and caste society separated the owners of property from the penniless poor has been narrowed down. In older ages the journeyman had such a low pay that he could hardly lay by something and, if he nevertheless did so, he could only keep his savings by hoarding and hiding a few coins. Under capitalism his competence makes saving possible, and there are institutions that enable him to invest his funds in business. A not inconsiderable amount of the capital employed in American industries is the counterpart of the savings of employees. In acquiring savings deposits, insurance policies, bonds and also common stock, wage earners and salaried people are themselves earning interest and dividends and thereby, in the terminology of Marxism, are exploiters.

The common man is directly interested in the flowering of business not only as a consumer and as an employee, but also as an investor. There prevails a tendency to efface to some extent the once sharp difference between those who own factors of production and those who do not. But, of course, this trend can only develop where the market economy is not sabotaged by allegedly social policies. The welfare state with its methods of easy money, credit expansion and undisguised inflation continually takes bites out of all claims payable in units of the nation's legal tender.

The self-styled champions of the common man are still guided by the obsolete idea that a policy that favors the debtors at the expense of the creditors is very beneficial to the majority of the people. Their inability to comprehend the essential characteristics of the market economy manifests itself also in their failure to see the obvious fact that those whom they feign to aid are creditors in their capacity as savers, policy holders, and owners of bonds.

7.

The distinctive principle of Western social philosophy is individualism. It aims at the creation of a sphere in which the individual is free to think, to choose, and to act without being restrained by the interference of the social apparatus of coercion and oppression, the State. All the spiritual and material achievements of Western civilization were the result of the operation of this idea of liberty.

This doctrine and the policies of individualism and of capitalism, its application to economic matters, do not need any apologists or propagandists. The achievements speak for themselves.

The case for capitalism and private property rests, apart from other considerations, also upon the incomparable efficiency of its productive effort. It is this efficiency that makes it possible for capitalistic business to support a rapidly increasing population at a continually improving standard of living. The resulting progressive prosperity of the masses creates a social environment in which the exceptionally gifted individuals are free to give to their fellow-citizens all they are able to give. The social system of private property and limited government is the only system that tends to debarbarize all those who have the innate capacity to acquire personal culture.

It is a gratuitous pastime to belittle the material achievements of capitalism by observing that there are things that are more essential for mankind than bigger and speedier motorcars, and homes equipped with central heating, air conditioning, refrigerators, washing machines, and television sets. There certainly are such higher and nobler pursuits. But they are higher and nobler precisely because they cannot be aspired to by any external effort but require the individual's personal determination and exertion. Those levelling this reproach against capitalism display a rather crude and materialistic view in assuming that moral and spiritual culture could be built either by the government or by the organization of production activities.

All that these external factors can achieve in this regard is to bring about an environment and a competence which offers the individuals the opportunity to work at their own personal perfection and edification. It is not the fault of capitalism that the masses prefer a boxing match to a performance of Sophocles' Antigone, jazz music to Beethoven symphonies, and comics to poetry. But it is certain that while pre-capitalistic conditions as they still prevail in the much greater part of the world makes these good things accessible only to a small minority of people, capitalism gives to the many a favorable chance of striving after them.

From whatever angle one may look at capitalism there is no reason to lament the passing of the allegedly good old days. Still less is it justified to long for the totalitarian utopias, whether of the Nazi or of the Soviet type.

We are inaugurating tonight the ninth meeting of the Mont Pelerin Society. It is fitting to remember on this occasion that meetings of this kind in which opinions opposed to those of the majority of our contemporaries and to those of their governments are advanced and are possible only in the climate of liberty and freedom that is the most precious mark of Western civilization. Let us hope that this right to dissent will never disappear.

Ludwig von Mises presented Liberty & Property as a lecture to the ninth meeting of The Mont Pelerin Society, held in Princeton, New Jersey, on 8 September 1958. Permission to reprint was granted by the Mises Institute.

5

Honour the entrepreneur and grow rich

Prior to 1800, most people lived subsistence existences. Dirt poor, their lives a drudgery, they suffered high rates of child mortality, starvation in poor seasons and ever-present violence. Then it changed. Beginning in Holland and the Anglosphere[29] and then spreading to many other nations and cultures, many societies became free and affluent.

Detailed information about this can be found in Max Rosser's *Our World in Data*. You will find a series of graphs showing a hundred years of world growth at the end of the book.

Here is how Max Rosser tells it from a United Kingdom perspective. [30]

Economic history is a very simple story. It is a story that has only two parts: The first part is the very long time in which the average person was very poor and human societies achieved no economic growth to change this.

Incomes remained almost unchanged over a period of several centuries when compared to the increase in incomes over the last 2 centuries. Life too changed remarkably little. What people used as shelter, food, clothing, energy supply, their light source stayed very similar for a very long time. Almost all that ordinary people used and consumed in the 17th century would have been very familiar to people living a thousand or even a couple of thousand years earlier. Average incomes (as measured by GDP per capita) in England between the year 1270 and 1650 were £1,051 when measured in today's prices.

---

29   UK, USA, Australia, New Zealand and Canada.
30   https://ourworldindata.org/economic-growth

The second part is much shorter, it encompasses only the last few generations and is radically different from the first part, it is a time in which the income of the average person grew immensely – from an average of £1051 incomes per person per year increased to over £30,000 a 29-fold increase in prosperity. This means an average person in the UK today has a higher income in two weeks than an average person in the past had in an entire year. Since the total sum of incomes is the total sum of production this also means that the production of the average person in two weeks today is equivalent to the production of the average person in an entire year in the past. There is just one truly important event in the economic history of the world, the onset of economic growth. This is the one transformation that changed everything.

What makes some nations rich and others poor? Why are resource-rich Tanzania and Argentina poor, while resource-poor Singapore, Hong Kong and Switzerland are rich? Why is there such a great disparity in wealth between adjacent countries with similar cultures, such as the former East and West Germany, North and South Korea, China and Taiwan, or Nogales Arizona in USA and Nogales Sonara in Mexico? The average South Korean lives 26 more years, and earns 15 times what they did in 1955, whereas for the average North Korean longevity and earnings have not changed. Why are the countries of North America so much more prosperous than those in South America? Why has Botswana thrived and but not Zimbabwe nor the Congo? Why are formerly prosperous population centres such as Baghdad, Venice, and Florence not as well-off today? Why was there an economic boom in China under Deng Xiaoping?

The reasons are complex, and the factors interact. Prosperity is like a jigsaw puzzle. There are many pieces that contribute to the result; some are more important than the others.

In *Guns, Germs and Steel* (1997), American scientist Jared Diamond posited that the fate of nations all began due to geographical good fortune. Nations with arable crops (wheat, barley, maize) and domesticable animals (cows, sheep, goats, pigs, chickens) thrived. In the eighteenth century, economist Adam Smith identified that labour productivity could be improved if everyone specialised in what they were good at and traded their produce with others. Leonard Read (see chapter 2) explained how the price mechanism enabled the division of labour to work in practice, with millions of people collaborating, blissfully unaware of the end-product. Max Weber argued that the protestant ethic of frugality, hard work and thrift, together with the religious notion that man had a calling and was obligated to use his talents appropriately, created the environment for capitalism to thrive.

Many other factors are significant, too. These include:

- The granting of civil liberties, such as the right to own private property, the advent of legally enforceable contracts, and the rights to choose one's occupation and to form voluntary associations (especially businesses).
- Changing social values on the dignity of work and respect for the entrepreneur.
- The availability of cheap sources of energy – coal, oil, and gas.
- Accumulated capital and the availability of infrastructure, resources, ideas, and institutions.
- Urbanisation, which made it easier for people to interact.
- Societies that permitted women into the paid workforce doubled the available talent.

The more we diversify as consumers and specialise as producers, the more prosperous we become as individuals and nations. It is the entrepreneurs who drive this economic process. They back their judgement and risk their time and their capital to create the goods and services that they perceive consumers want. In doing so, they need to be confident that they can keep the results of their efforts and not have their wealth confiscated by the state.

As Acemoglu & Robinson explain in *Why Nations Fail: The origins of power, prosperity and poverty* (2012):

> *Secure private property rights are central, since only those with such rights will be willing to invest and increase productivity. A businessman who expects his output to be stolen, expropriated, or entirely taxed away will have little incentive to work, let alone incentive to undertake investments and innovations.*

Or as Matt Ridley put it succinctly in *The Rational Optimist: How prosperity evolves* (2010): "Merchants and craftsmen make prosperity: chiefs, priests and thieves fritter it away."

Free-market economies flourished in the 100 years prior to the First World War. Both populations and prosperity grew at amazing rates. In the United Kingdom, the population increased four-fold and GDP per capita doubled. In the United States, the population increased 12-fold and GDP per capita grew by 350 per cent. Over the past one hundred years, all over the world, nations have thrived by adopting free-market economies and democratic forms of government. It happened not just in the Anglosphere, but also in countries as diverse as Denmark, Sweden, Switzerland, Singapore, Japan, South Korea, Taiwan, and Hong Kong. In the past thirty years, there has also been rapid economic and population growth in former Soviet bloc countries such as Lithuania, Estonia, Latvia, and Kazakhstan, and Eastern European countries such as Czechia, Poland, Slovakia, and Hungary.[31]

What changed in the latter part of the eighteenth century? The popular theories are that it was due to material causes - exploitation by colonialists, the use of slave labour, the theft of gold, even international trade. These miss the point. Such factors existed in many societies before 1800 without making the dramatic changes we have seen in the past two hundred years.

McCloskey argues that the difference was a change in attitude. In the days when the aristocracy felt that trade was demeaning and the Church believed that only the priests should read and interpret the holy scriptures, economic activity was stymied. Significant change came when people began to honour the entrepreneur. Then it became acceptable to be in business, to innovate and to retain the rewards of hard work and risk-taking investment. I think she is right.

To be successful, entrepreneurs must industriously research what their customers want and value, and then innovate and invest to create products and services that are superior to competitive offerings. The more successful they are, the more we, as consumers, benefit. It is in our own interest to honour the entrepreneur. That is the way to ensure our own prosperity.

---

31   See Appendix I One hundred years of growth worldwide

Deirdre McCloskey (1942–)

Deirdre Nansen McCloskey is a distinguished professor emerita in economics and history, and professor emerita in English and communication, at the University of Illinois at Chicago, in the United States. She was raised in an academic environment. Her mother played tennis socially with Paul Samuelson, whose textbook misled a generation of economics students.

Trained at Harvard University in the 1960s as an economist, McCloskey has published twenty books and some 400 academic articles on economic theory, economic history, philosophy, rhetoric, statistical theory, feminism, ethics and the law.

Her most recent books are *Why Liberalism Works: How true liberal values produce a freer, more equal, prosperous world for all* (Yale University Press, 2019) and with Art Carden *Leave Me Alone and I'll Make You Rich: The Bourgeois Deal* (University of Chicago Press, 2020).

In 2019, the Chicago Press published a third edition of her classic manual on style, *Economical Writing,* and a 20th-anniversary re-issuing of *Crossing: A Transgender Memoir.*

Her major work is the bourgeois era trilogy:

* *The Bourgeois Virtues: Ethics for an age of commerce (2006)*

* *Bourgeois Dignity: Why economics can't explain the modern world (2010)*

- *Bourgeois Equality: How ideas, not capital or institutions, enriched the world (2016).*

In the final volume, *Bourgeois Equality,* McCloskey argues that the accidents of reformation and revolt in northwestern Europe in the period 1517–1789 led to a new liberty and dignity for commoners, which led in turn to an explosion of *trade-tested betterment.* This delivered the exponential increases in prosperity since 1800.

In the second book in the trilogy, *Bourgeois Dignity,* McCloskey had shown that materialist explanations – slavery, colonialism and exploitation – are insufficient to explain the Great Enrichment.

Moreover, the Great Enrichment did not corrupt our immortal souls. The inaugural book in the trilogy, *The Bourgeois Virtues,* established that *innovism* (McCloskey's preferred term for capitalism) is ethical. It rewards business behaviour that is honest, fair, civil and compassionate.

The trilogy looks forward to a world of universal dignity and prosperity, created by liberal innovism.

> *Liberty and Dignity Explain the Modern World* is a short summary of these ideas. In it, McCloskey explains that it was human dignity and liberty that caused our enrichment, and with it our modern prosperity and freedom.

Liberty and Dignity Explain the Modern World

Deirdre McCloskey

A change in how people honored markets and innovation caused the Industrial Revolution – and what is more significant a subsequent Great Enrichment, and then the modern world. The old conventional wisdom, by contrast, has no place for attitudes, and no place for liberal thought. The old materialist story says that the Industrial Revolution (at which it stops thinking) came from material causes, from investment or theft, from higher saving rates or from imperialism. You've heard it: "Europe is rich because of its empires"; "The United States was built on the backs of slaves"; "China is getting rich because of foreign trade."

But what if the Great Enrichment, 1800 to the present, was sparked instead by changes in the way people thought, and especially by how they thought about each other? Suppose steam engines and computers came from a new honor for innovators – not from piling brick on brick, or dead African on dead African?

Economists and historians are starting to recognise the big shift by around 1800 in how Westerners thought about commerce and innovation, and now the Chinese and Indians. People had to start accepting "creative destruction", the new idea that replaces the old. It's like music. A new band gets a new idea in rock music and replaces the old if enough people freely adopt the new. If the old music is thought to be worse, it is "destroyed" by the creativity. In the same way, electric lights "destroyed" kerosene lamps, and computers "destroyed" typewriters. To our good.

The correct history goes like this: Until the Dutch (around 1600) or the

English (around 1700) changed their thinking, you got honor in only two ways, by being a soldier or being a priest, in the castle or in the church. People who merely bought and sold things for a living, or innovated, were scorned as sinful cheaters, more or less worldwide, and especially in Europe. A jailer in the 1200s rejected a rich man's pleas for mercy: "Come, master Annaud Teisseire, you have wallowed in such opulence! ... How could you be without sin"?

In 1800 the average income per person per day all over the planet, I have noted, was, in present-day money, anything from $1 to $5. Call it an average of $3 per day. Sometimes $2. Imagine living in present day Rio or Athens or Johannesburg on $2 or $3 a day. (Some people do, even now, but very few even now in most cities, the cities which nowadays contain half the world's population.)

That's three-fourths of a cappuccino in Starbucks. It was and is appalling.[32]

Then something changed, in Holland first and then in England. The revolutions and reformations of Europe, 1517 to 1789, gave voice to ordinary people as against the priests and aristocrats. Northwestern Europeans and in the long run many others came to admire entrepreneurs like Ben Franklin and Andrew Carnegie and Nikola Tesla and Bill Gates. The middle class started to be viewed as good, and started to be allowed to do good, and to do well. People adopted "innovism" – a better word than the misleading "capitalism", to describe what happened 1700 or so to the present. People signed on to a Bourgeois Deal that has characterized now-wealthy places such as Britain and Sweden and Hong Kong ever since: "Let me innovate and make piles and piles of money in the short run, and in the long run I'll make *you* rich".

And that's what happened. Starting in the 1770s with Franklin's lightning rod and Watt's steam engine, and going mad in the 1800s, and still more mad in the 1900s and 2000s, The West, which for centuries had lagged behind China and Islam, became astoundingly innovative. Give the

---

32 I think she is saying that it is the poverty that is appalling, not the Starbuck's coffee.

middle class – and the workers climbing up into it, and the workers themselves whether or not they climb – dignity and liberty for the first time in human history and here's what you get: the steam engine, the automatic textile loom, the assembly line, the symphony orchestra, the railway, the corporation, abolitionism, the steam printing press, cheap paper, wide literacy, the modern newspaper, cheap steel, cheap plate glass, the modern university, sewers, clean water, reinforced concrete, the women's movement, the electric light, the elevator, the automobile, petroleum, vacations in Yellowstone, plastics, a third of a million new English-language books a year, hybrid corn, penicillin, the airplane, clean urban air, civil rights, open-heart surgery, and the computer. The result was that, uniquely in history, the ordinary people, and especially the very poor, were made much, much better off. The Bourgeois Deal paid for it. The poorest 5 percent of Americans are now about as well off in air-conditioning and automobiles as the richest 5 percent of South Asians – thought the South Asians are rising too.

We're seeing the same shift play out in China and India, 40 percent of the world's population. The big economic story of our times is not the Great Recession of 2007-2009, unpleasant though it was. Now it's over. The big story is that the Chinese in 1978 and then the Indians in 1991 began to adopt liberal ideas in their economies and came to welcome creative destruction. And it's far from over. Now their goods and services per person are quadrupling in every generation. In the numerous places that had long adopted bourgeois liberty and dignity, the average person makes and consumes over $100 per day, as against the $3 per day in the same dollars of recent purchasing power from which we all came. And the figure doesn't take full account of the radical improvement in quality of many things, from electric lights to antibiotics to theories of economics. Young people in Japan and Norway and Italy are, conservatively measured (that is, without full corrections for quality), around thirty times better off in material circumstances than their great-great-great-great-great-grandparents. All the other leaps into the modern world – more democracy, the liberation of women, improved life expectancy, more education, more spiritual growth, more artistic explosion – depend on the Great Enrichment.

The Great Enrichment was so big, so unprecedented, that it's impossible to see it as coming out of routine causes, such as trade or exploitation or investment or imperialism. Economic science of an orthodox character is good at explaining routine. Yet all such routines had already occurred on a big scale in China and the Ottoman Empire, in Rome and South Asia. Slavery was common in the Middle East, trade was large in India, the investment in Chinese canals and Roman roads was immense. Yet no Great Enrichment happened.

Something must be deeply wrong, therefore, with explanations of the usual, material, economic sort. Depending on economic materialism to explain the modern world, whether left-wing historical materialism or right-wing orthodox economics, is mistaken.

Ideas of human dignity and liberty did the trick, making the inventions and then investments profitable for entrepreneurs and the nation. As economic historian Joel Mokyr puts it, "economic change in all periods depends, more than most economists think, on what people believe". It was ideas, "rhetoric", that caused our enrichment, and with it our modern riches and liberties.

This article was first published in 2011 as a chapter in *The Morality of Capitalism: What your professors won't tell you,* edited by Tom Palmer. It has recently been reprinted in McCloskey's *Why Liberalism Works; How true liberal values produce a freer, more equal, prosperous world for all* (2019). Permission to reprint was granted by the Atlas Network.

6

The inhibiting ideologies

It would seem that no advanced civilisation has yet developed without a government which saw its chief aim in the protection of private property, but that again and again the further evolution and growth to which this gave rise was halted by a 'strong' government. Government strong enough to protect individuals against the violence of their fellows made possible the evolution of an increasingly complex order of spontaneous and voluntary cooperation. Sooner or later, however, they tend to abuse that power and to suppress the freedom they had earlier secured in order to enforce their own presumably greater wisdom and not to allow 'social institutions to develop in a haphazard manner' (to take a characteristic expression that is found under the heading of 'social engineering' in the Fontana/Harper Dictionary of Modern Thought. (1977).[33]

The history of the world over the past two hundred years provides clear evidence that societies which have embraced liberal democratic principles – individual rights, private property, the rule of law, and representative government– have thrived. Recent analysis by the Canadian think tank, The Fraser Institute, confirms this in its snapshot of the world today.

The *Human Freedom Index 2021* [34] assesses 165 countries and measures the degree to which the policies and institutions of countries are supportive of economic freedom. The top places went to Switzerland, New Zealand, Denmark, Estonia, Ireland, Canada and Finland (tied for 6th), Australia, Sweden and Luxembourg. Other interesting results include United Kingdom (14), Germany, Japan and the United States (tied at 15), Taiwan (19), Chile (28), Hong Kong (30), South Korea (31),

33   Hayek (1988) p. 32
34   You can download this from www.fraserinstitute.com

France (34), Argentina (74), South Africa (77), Brazil (78), Mexico (93), India (119), Nigeria (123), Russia (126), Turkey (139), China (150), Saudi Arabia (155), Iran (160), Venezuela (164), and Syria (165).

The report draws our attention to the significant correlation between freedom and affluence.

> *Jurisdictions in the top quartile of freedom enjoy a significantly higher average per capita income ($48,748) than those in other quartiles; the average per capita income in the least free quartile is $11,259.*

Yet despite all this evidence, our rulers revert to romantic notions of the will of the people and central economic planning. Socialism was the dominant political ideology of the twentieth century, practised as communism in the East and as the social democratic welfare state in the West.

In the United States, Roosevelt's New Deal introduced regulation of industry and agriculture together with price and wage controls which extended the Great Depression for a decade. [35] A few of the programs "like the industrial union legislation, universal social insurance, Fannie Mae, bank deposit insurance, and farm price supports, lived on to cast a heavy and debilitating shadow over the distant future."[36] Johnson's well-intentioned Great Society programs spent millions replacing slums with public housing and creating public sector jobs, but they had negligible impact on poverty and serious adverse consequences on the lives of the communities targeted.[37]

The European Union has been constrained by the regulatory mindset of its bureaucrats. For a good understanding of this, see *Brexit: The Movie* – a 2016 British documentary film written and directed by Martin Durkin, advocating the withdrawal of the United Kingdom from the European Union, which is available on YouTube.

The exemplar of the social democratic welfare state has been Sweden.

---

35   Brown et al. (1974)
36   Stockman, D. (2013) p. 140
37   Shlaes, A. (2019)

But it turns out that the Swedish model failed too. Let us review a little history.

In 1850, Sweden was one of the poorest countries in the world. Over the next hundred years, income increased eight times and the population doubled. Infant mortality fell from 15 to 2 per cent and life expectancy increased by 28 years. By 1950, Sweden was the fourth richest country in the world.

The benefits that began in 1850 had their genesis in the work of Anders Chydenius whose advocacy of a free market and a minimal state preceded Adam Smith by eleven years. His support for freedom of the press in 1766 had a crucial influence on Sweden's economic development. In the early nineteenth century, it enabled Lars Johan Hierta to establish an evening newspaper, Aftonbladet, in which he promoted his views of classical liberalism – especially the right to private property and equal treatment before the law. This led to significant practical changes.

Between 1849 and 1865, joint-stock company law was introduced, banks were allowed to be established and interest rates were deregulated. Regulations restricting the iron and timber industries were lifted, the guild system was abolished, and it became easier to start a business. Immigration and emigration were permitted, education became more universally available, and women were permitted to own and inherit property, be educated and to have a career.

These changes created a fruitful environment for entrepreneurs. Most of Sweden's great companies were established around the turn of the century, including Atlas Copco (1873), L.M. Ericsson (1876), ASEA (1883), Alfa Laval (1883), Scania (1891), AGA (1904), SKF (1907), and Electrolux (1910).

Sweden thrived. It also benefitted by staying out of two world wars.

The Social Democratic Party came to power in 1932 and dominated Swedish politics for most of the rest of the century. They began cautiously, maintaining capitalist institutions, and working to keep big business and the middle class on side. By 1950, taxes were still lower and the public sector smaller than comparable countries.

It was later, in the fifties, sixties and seventies, that welfare state policies were implemented. Between 1950 and 1980, public spending rose from 19 to 60 per cent of GDP. And that is when it all started to unravel. The scope of government benefits expanded, rigid labour market regulations were introduced, stagnating sectors of the economy were propped up and taxes dramatically increased. Growth rates declined. The currency had to be devalued. By 1990, the public sector had increased by over a million employees, but not one net private sector job had been created in forty years. Compared to the USA, by the end of the 1990s, the median household income was two-thirds and the proportion of the adult population with a bachelor's degree was about half.

There have been other adverse social effects. There has been a decline in the institution of marriage; a high proportion of adults now live alone. Children are brought up by the state not their parents. Crime rates have increased, particularly violent crime. Swedish- born academic, Per Bylund, bemoans the loss of bourgeois virtues. Within two generations, he writes, Swedes went from being a proud, hard-working and self-reliant people to a nation of immature, irresponsible, needy, spoiled and utterly demanding individuals. [38]

Sweden's wealth in the middle of the twentieth century was due to the intellectual input of men such as Chydenius and Hierta, and the operation of a free market economy from 1850 to 1950. While the Social Democrats kept a free market economy in place the country remained wealthy. But when they thought that they could squander its capital on cradle to grave welfare they quickly destroyed everything. It took less than 30 years to drop from the fourth richest country in the world to the fourteenth.

In recent years, Sweden has reduced taxes, privatized sectors of the economy and reformed its pension system. It is publicly honouring Chydenius and Hierta. Things are looking up. They have recognised that the Swedish model failed. [39]

Socialist ideologies have proved a handbrake on progress, more so in countries which had already, like Sweden, achieved a degree of success. Most people find this difficult to acknowledge.

We are ready to accept almost any explanation of the present crisis in our civilization except one: that the present state of the world may be the result of genuine error on our part and that the pursuit of some of our most cherished ideals has apparently produced results utterly different from those we expected. [40]

The beneficiaries of the popular socialist and welfare systems that have dominated the democracies of developed nations since the Second World War have not been the poor and the disadvantaged. Rather, the beneficiaries have been elites with political influence who could capture and manipulate the state to their own benefit.

It also has had a debilitating effect on the moral fibre of our societies. Yuval Levin, Hertog Fellow at the Ethics and Public Policy Centre in Washington D.C, clearly articulates what is wrong:

---

38 Bylund, P. (2006)
39 Fenwick, P. (2016)
40 Hayek, F.A. (1944/2007) p. 65

Moreover, because all citizens – not only the poor – become recipients of benefits, people in the middle class come to approach their government as claimants, not as self-governing citizens, and to approach the social safety net not as a great majority of givers eager to make sure that a small minority of recipients are spared from devastating poverty, but as a mass of dependents demanding what they are owed. It is hard to imagine an ethic better suited to undermining the moral basis of a free society. [41]

All over the world, people are becoming freer and more affluent. But it would happen faster if it were not constrained by intellectuals, politicians and bureaucrats who think they know better.

---

41   Levin, Y. (2011)

Matt Ridley (1958–)

Matthew White Ridley, the fifth Viscount Ridley, is a member of the British aristocracy. His family has been contributing to British intellectual and political life for generations. He is the ninth Matt Ridley to serve in the British parliament. Ridley's great-grandfather, Sir Edwin Lutyens, was the leading architect in the design of New Delhi in the early twentieth century; his great-great-great-great-grandfather, Dudley Marjoribanks, first Baron Tweedmouth, created the golden retriever breed. He is married to the neuroscientist professor Anya Hurlbert. They have two children and live on the family estate at Blagdon near Newcastle-upon-Tyne, in the north of England.

Educated at Eton College and Oxford University, Ridley achieved a first-class honours degree and a doctorate in zoology, then worked for *The Economist* for nine years as a science writer, as a Washington correspondent and editor. Nowadays, he writes regular columns for the *Wall Street Journal* and *The Times*.

Matt Ridley has written many books, including:

- *The Origins of Virtue: Human instincts and the evolution of cooperation* (1998)
- *Genome: The autobiography of a species in 23 chapters* (2000)
- *The Red Queen: Sex and the evolution of human nature* (2003)

- *The Agile Gene: How nature turns on nurture* (2004)
- *The Rational Optimist: How prosperity evolves* (2010)
- *Francis Crick: Discoverer of the genetic code* (2011)
- *The Evolution of Everything: How new ideas emerge* (2016)
- *How Innovation Works: And why it flourishes in freedom* (2020).

In *The Rational Optimist*, Ridley argues that human prosperity is due to our willingness to trade with strangers. This enables the division of labour and permits us to specialise, to work on the things we are good at. In turn, that encourages us to innovate, to create tools, machines and processes that make our production more efficient. We trade ideas, too. We learn skills from experts and build on what has gone before, so a communal intelligence develops. Prosperity increases exponentially. Trading relationships depend on trust and building reputations. If you can be trusted, then more people will deal with you. Where trade flourishes, so do other virtues. Cities and towns provide more opportunity for interactions, for innovators to meet and share ideas, than rural areas, so people tend to move to the cities where they can trade and be prosperous. Creativity and compassion were most evident in the great commercial cities of the past, and it is the same today.

Ridley summarises our current situation as follows:

> *Human beings are not only wealthier, but healthier, happier, cleaner, cleverer, kinder, freer, more peaceful and more equal than they have ever been. This is because the source of human innovation is, and has been for 100,000 years, not the individual inspiration through reason but collective intelligence evolving by trial and error resulting from the sharing of ideas through exchange and specialization. The secret of human prosperity is that everyone is working for everybody else.*

When Ideas Have Sex, Ridley's prologue to *The Rational Optimist*, became a 16-minute TED talk, and is available on YouTube where it has been viewed 2.5 million times.

> *On 9 November 1989, the Berlin Wall fell, and the communist experiment was over. Established with much hope and intellectual support, it had delivered poverty, destroyed trust among its citizens, and terrorised, censored and imprisoned those who disagreed with the party line.*

On the eve of the centenary of the Bolshevik revolution, which ushered in the communist experiment, Matt Ridley reviews the horrors of the 100 years of failure of this ideology.

A Century of Marxism-Leninism

Matt Ridley

Human beings can be remarkably dense. The practice of bloodletting, as a medical treatment, persisted despite centuries of abundant evidence that it did more harm than good. The practice of communism, or political bloodletting as it should perhaps be known, whose centenary in the Bolshevik revolution is reached this year, likewise needs no more tests. It does more harm than good every time. Nationalised, planned, one-party rule benefits nobody, let alone the poor.

The diseases that Marxism-Leninism was intended to treat, poverty and inequality, were ancient scourges just beginning to fade, even in Russia. Higher living standards were starting to reach ordinary people, rather than just the feudal elite, for the first time. Radicals had long seen government as the problem, not the solution: that to enrich the masses required liberating people from kings and priests.

Along came Karl Marx with essentially the opposite suggestion: a powerful state creating wealth, distributed from each according to his ability to each according to his need, as a result of which classes would disappear and with them, eventually, the state itself.

The progressive Left rather suddenly fell in love with the idea of expanding, rather than limiting, state power. It was in such a good cause. Unfortunately, the wealth never materialised and the state, far from withering away, became tyrannical.

Russia's Bolsheviks, seizing power in a coup after the fall of the tsar, set a pattern that would be repeated again and again during the following century. A communist party takes power on behalf of the people, outlaws all other parties, holds no elections and after a sanguineous power struggle is soon dominated by one man. Famine results from the destruction of incentives inherent in the collectivisation of agriculture. Millions die. The nationalisation of all commerce and the cessation of most foreign trade result in shortages of consumer goods.

The leader becomes paranoid and kills a lot of people, especially independently minded ones, in purges. More are imprisoned without trial or charge. A secret police grows powerful. The regime destroys free speech but is excused and praised by left-leaning sympathisers in Western democracies.

Living standards stagnate or fall, except for those of the elite, who live a privileged existence. Many people try to flee.

Communism was not unique in ruling through violence. Fascism, founded by an ardent socialist, Benito Mussolini, and German National Socialism, pursuing racial rather than class-based collectivism, were at least as bad, though they ended up killing fewer – not for lack of trying.

But from this distance they are all manifestations of the same phenomenon: centrally planned dictatorship justified as popular rule. Hitler's bombers over London in 1940 burnt Soviet fuel.

In 1949, China repeated the Russian experiment with the same result. Mao Zedong managed to kill even more people, probably 45 million in the four years of the Great Leap Forward, through forced collectivisation and selling food to Russia in exchange for nuclear technology. When that did not work, and he began to lose his grip on power, he embarked on a purge of the entire country, called the Cultural Revolution, plunging his people into abject poverty while himself living like an emperor.

In 1959, Cuba tried Marxism-Leninism with a similar outcome: 5000 people executed, an unknown number imprisoned for dissent and tens of thousands dead after trying to escape on makeshift rafts. Cuba's GDP per capita was about the same as South Korea's in 1959. Today, South Korea's is five times higher.

In 1962, Burma followed suit when Ne Win seized power and set out to create a "socialist state". He introduced one-party rule, nationalised business and isolated the country from world trade, while imprisoning and executing perceived rivals. He impoverished the country while its neighbours prospered.

In 1974, it was Benin's turn for the purges and oppression. The economy stagnated for a quarter of a century. Elsewhere in Africa, the Republic of the Congo and Zimbabwe also tried communism, Robert Mugabe having come to power (lest we forget) as an enthusiastic Marxist-Leninist.

East Germany had to build a wall to stop people escaping. Vietnam, like Cuba, sent thousands to sea in leaky boats. Cambodia deserves special mention for the thoroughness with which it stuck to Marx's plan of "sweeping aside" the bourgeoisie. As head of the Khmer Rouge, Pol Pot enslaved the entire population on collective farms, his thugs clubbing or starving any who showed less than total obedience, so that from 1975 to 1979 approximately 1.7 million people were killed.

North Korea managed to turn communism into a feudal dynasty of unparalleled paranoia, which not only executes supposed dissidents in unusually gruesome ways but managed to starve millions of its citizens during the 1990s, a time when the rest of the world was feeding itself ever more abundantly.

Oil-rich Venezuela has ruined itself through socialism, creating shortages of loo paper and soap. It's been said that if they tried communism in the Sahara, there would soon be a shortage of sand.

Those communist countries that discovered economic growth, notably Vietnam and China after Mao, did so by abandoning nationalisation of the means of production, the very core of the Marxist prescription. They were exceptions that proved the rule.

Need I go on? Communism has killed on average a million people a year for a century, far more than any other ism, let alone what Marxists call "capitalism", and the rest of us call freedom.

The first communists meant well. Their crime was to bet the farm on an untried idea and then, when it failed (as Lenin's half-hearted New Economic Policy conceded), to be pig-headedly insensitive to the negative empirical data coming back from the experiment.

Like bloodletting medics, they elevated a principle into a dogma, with no regard to human suffering, in spite of overwhelming evidence.

This article originally appeared in *The Times* on 2 January 2017 and subsequently on Matt Ridley's blog https://www.rationaloptimist.com/blog/communisms-centenary/. Permission to reprint was granted by Matt Ridley.

7

Tolerance in a pluralist society

My father was Catholic, my mother Protestant. There was a term for it at the time: a mixed marriage. When I was growing up in the 1950s, there were serious prejudices against Catholics. They were often denied employment by professional firms and refused admission to certain clubs. My father was the first Catholic admitted to the Geelong Legacy club, a charity that looks after the families of deceased servicemen. At his admission, Dad's best mate, Cliff Cooke, with typical understated Australian humour, said that Frank was 'Okay, despite the fact that he was a Catholic'! A few years later, Dad was elected president of the club.

In Canberra, government departments were divided on sectarian lines: Treasury staff were typically Protestant, while tax office staff were Catholic. In 1955, the Australian Labor Party (ALP) split over attitudes to communism, with the Catholics forming the Democratic Labor Party (DLP). This kept the ALP out of office until Gough Whitlam led it to victory in 1972. In contrast, in recent years, both major political parties have led by men, Tony Abbot and Bill Shorten, who had been trained by the Jesuits. No-one thought anything of it. Without any grand pronouncements from the Pope or the Archbishop of Canterbury, these past antagonisms had dissipated.

Formerly, many societies shared common cultural and religious beliefs. Nowadays, most societies are pluralist. "The political culture of a democratic society is always marked by a diversity of opposing and irreconcilable religious, philosophical and moral doctrines." [42] We should realise and accept that such views can be reasonably held. Consequently, we shall often need to embrace conflicting values, to tolerate others'

---

42   Rawls, J. (1993). p. 3

views even if we do not agree with them. If we wish to change others' views it should be done by persuasion, not coercion.

On the other hand, it is natural for us to want to socialise with people who share our views and our values. As individuals, and as societies, we focus initially on members of our own family. As we mature, as we become more civilised, our circle of friends grows in concentric rings to include neighbours; members of the local church, school or community associations; friends we make at school or university or at the firms where we work; people with whom we play golf or tennis or bridge; or who barrack for Collingwood, or who don't. These are the people we trust. Significantly, we also happily associate with the people with whom we trade. We trust them, too. Sometimes, we might invite them into the inner rings and introduce them to our closer friends.

When Cliff Cooke introduced my dad to his club, his message was, 'This fellow is okay once you get to know him'. If we aspire to tolerance, we need to encourage citizens to be involved with the widest possible cross-section of our society. This is what I call *the principle of multiple associations*. The wider our circle of friends and acquaintances, the more tolerant we become. If we socialise only with the same few then we will not be comfortable with people from outside our narrow group. But if we meet different people at work, at play, at community functions, at sporting events and in volunteer organisations, then we will realise that *most people are okay once you get to know them*. If we make an effort to meet strangers, we will not fear outsiders, and we will not ostracise and abuse those we do not know. We shall become mature and tolerant.

To facilitate our social activities, we form clubs and associations. There will be rules, defined by the existing membership, to determine who can become a new member. That is their prerogative. It is not something to be criticised as intolerance. It is reasonable for members to exclude the uncouth or those who do not meet the objectives of the club. If the rules are restrictive, then there will be few who qualify, and the club will remain small. Larger clubs need to be more accommodating. My wife is a member of the Lyceum Club. It is a club for professional women. There can be no objection that the club requires women to have a university degree or that it excludes men from membership. Such criteria are integral to the club's purpose.

Furthermore, being competitive is not intolerant. My mother always exhorted me to do my best. I demanded the same from my sons and my staff. It is natural and good to strive to achieve and make the most of our talents. Consequently, we may promote ourselves and our organisations as superior. Provided they are, of course. Unjustified bravado is just irritating. Also, we need to restrain ourselves from verbally abusing opponents who can perform better than we can. That is crass. We need to develop the maturity to be able to accept that some people are wealthier, cleverer, more skilful, more successful, or can run faster, or kick more goals for the opposing team. Once we accept this, we can act without rancour.

Stephen Pinker provides pause for thought:

> *The human moral sense can also work at cross-purposes to our well-being. People demonize those they disagree with, attributing differences of opinion to stupidity and dishonesty. For every misfortune they seek a scapegoat. They see morality as a source of grounds for condemning rivals and mobilizing indignation against them. The grounds for condemnation may consist in the defendants' having harmed others, but they also may consist in having flouted custom, questioned authority, undermined tribal solidarity, or engaged in unclean sexual or dietary practices. People see violence as moral, not immoral; across the world and throughout history, more people have been murdered to mete out justice than to satisfy greed.[43]*

In the United States, the Civil War (1861–65) abolished slavery but not prejudice and violence. One hundred years later, African Americans were still treated as second-class citizens. They were segregated in schools and on public transport, and artificial restrictions limited their ability to vote. President Eisenhower signed the *Civil Rights Act of 1957*, which aimed to address these wrongs. But it was not just the law that had to change. For the law to be effective there had to be changes in attitude. From both sides.

The work of Dr Martin Luther King made a lasting contribution to this

---

43   Pinker, S. (2018). p. 26

change.

The King Centre, established in 1968 by his wife, Coretta Scott King, and now led by their daughter, Dr Bernice King, is continuing his work. Its mission is 'to empower people to create a just, humane, equitable and peaceful world by applying Dr. King's nonviolent philosophy and methodology'. The riots of 2019 in US cities following the death of George Floyd show that much work is still to be done and that not everyone agrees with King's non-violent strategy.

Dr Martin Luther King Jr (1929–1968)

Martin Luther King, Junior came from a comfortable middle-class family steeped in the tradition of the Southern Black ministry of the United States. His parents were college educated, and King's father had succeeded his maternal grandfather as pastor of the prestigious Ebenezer Baptist Church in Atlanta.

King attended segregated public schools in Georgia, graduating from high school at the age of fifteen. He received a Bachelor of Arts degree from Morehouse College in Atlanta, a Bachelor of Divinity from Crozer Theological Seminary in Pennsylvania, and a doctorate in systematic theology from Boston University.

In Boston, he met Coretta Scott, who was studying at the New England Conservatory of Music. They married in 1953 and had four children.

In 1954, Martin Luther King became pastor of the Dexter Avenue Baptist Church in Montgomery, Alabama. When Rosa Parks was arrested for violating the city's segregation law in December 1955 – she had refused to surrender her seat to a white passenger – King was chosen to lead the boycott of the transit system. Despite his home being destroyed by dynamite attacks and his family's safety being threatened, King held firm. A little over a year later, the Supreme Court of the United States declared that the laws requiring segregation on buses were unconstitutional. Black and white Americans could ride the buses as equals.

King led the American Civil Rights Movement from then until his assassination in 1968. Drawing on his Baptist roots and inspired by Mahatma Gandhi, he sought equality for African Americans through legal means, rhetoric and non-violent resistance. In the next decade, he travelled over 6 million miles and gave 2500 speeches. King was assaulted and arrested many times.

The discrimination against blacks was real and systemic. For instance, in 1964, only 6.7 per cent of eligible black citizens in Mississippi were registered to vote. In Alabama, King planned the drives for the registration of black voters and led a massive protest in Birmingham. Meanwhile, he wrote five books and numerous articles, including the inspiring 'Letter from Birmingham Jail'. King recognised that the problem for black people was not only race discrimination, but it was also poverty. He worked with Walter Reuther of the United Auto Workers union to influence both the Kennedy and Johnson administrations, and to organise the March on Washington for Jobs and Freedom.

King was awarded the Nobel Peace Prize (1964) and posthumously the Presidential Medal of Freedom (1977) and the Congressional Gold Medal (2003). A national holiday was declared in his honour.

> On 28 August 1963, Martin Luther King Jr addressed a crowd of 250,000 people at the Lincoln Memorial in Washington, D.C. King asked the people of the United States to honour their pledge to provide the unalienable rights of life, liberty and the pursuit of happiness to all its citizens – and not to deny these rights to African Americans.

> 'I Have a Dream' was indeed one of the great speeches of the 20th century.

I Have a Dream

Martin Luther King Jr

I am happy to join with you today in what will go down in history as the greatest demonstration for freedom in the history of our nation.

Five score years ago, a great American, in whose symbolic shadow we stand today, signed the Emancipation Proclamation. This momentous decree came as a great beacon light of hope to millions of Negro slaves who had been seared in the flames of withering injustice. It came as a joyous daybreak to end the long night of their captivity.

But one hundred years later, the Negro still is not free. One hundred years later, the life of the Negro is still sadly crippled by the manacles of segregation and the chains of discrimination. One hundred years later, the Negro lives on a lonely island of poverty in the midst of a vast ocean of material prosperity. One hundred years later, the Negro is still languished in the corners of American society and finds himself an exile in his own land. And so we've come here today to dramatize a shameful condition.

In a sense we've come to our nation's capital to cash a check. When the architects of our republic wrote the magnificent words of the Constitution and the Declaration of Independence, they were signing a promissory note to which every American was to fall heir. This note was a promise that all men, yes, black men as well as white men, would be guaranteed the "unalienable Rights" of "Life, Liberty and the pursuit of Happiness." It is obvious today that America has defaulted on this promissory note, insofar as her citizens of color are concerned. Instead of honoring this sacred obligation, America has given the Negro people a bad check, a check which has come back marked "insufficient funds."

But we refuse to believe that the bank of justice is bankrupt. We refuse to believe that there are insufficient funds in the great vaults of opportunity of this nation. And so, we've come to cash this check, a check that will give us upon demand the riches of freedom and the security of justice.

We have also come to this hallowed spot to remind America of the fierce urgency of Now. This is no time to engage in the luxury of cooling off or to take the tranquilizing drug of gradualism. Now is the time to make real the promises of democracy. Now is the time to rise from the dark and desolate valley of segregation to the sunlit path of racial justice. Now is the time to lift our nation from the quicksands of racial injustice to the solid rock of brotherhood. Now is the time to make justice a reality for all of God's children.

It would be fatal for the nation to overlook the urgency of the moment. This sweltering summer of the Negro's legitimate discontent will not pass until there is an invigorating autumn of freedom and equality. Nineteen sixty-three is not an end, but a beginning. And those who hope that the Negro needed to blow off steam and will now be content will have a rude awakening if the nation returns to business as usual. And there will be neither rest nor tranquillity in America until the Negro is granted his citizenship rights. The whirlwinds of revolt will continue to shake the foundations of our nation until the bright day of justice emerges.

But there is something that I must say to my people, who stand on the warm threshold which leads into the palace of justice: In the process of gaining our rightful place, we must not be guilty of wrongful deeds. Let us not seek to satisfy our thirst for freedom by drinking from the cup of bitterness and hatred. We must forever conduct our struggle on the high plane of dignity and discipline. We must not allow our creative protest to degenerate into physical violence. Again and again, we must rise to the majestic heights of meeting physical force with soul force.

The marvellous new militancy which has engulfed the Negro community must not lead us to a distrust of all white people, for many of our white brothers, as evidenced by their presence here today, have come to realize that their destiny is tied up with our destiny. And they have come to realize that their freedom is inextricably bound to our freedom.

We cannot walk alone.

And as we walk, we must make the pledge that we shall always march ahead.

We cannot turn back.

There are those who are asking the devotees of civil rights, "When will you be satisfied?" We can never be satisfied as long as the Negro is the victim of the unspeakable horrors of police brutality. We can never be satisfied as long as our bodies, heavy with the fatigue of travel, cannot gain lodging in the motels of the highways and the hotels of the cities. We cannot be satisfied as long as the negro's basic mobility is from a smaller ghetto to a larger one. We can never be satisfied as long as our children are stripped of their self-hood and robbed of their dignity by signs stating: "For Whites Only." We cannot be satisfied as long as a Negro in Mississippi cannot vote, and a Negro in New York believes he has nothing for which to vote. No, no, we are not satisfied, and we will not be satisfied until "justice rolls down like waters, and righteousness like a mighty stream."

I am not unmindful that some of you have come here out of great trials and tribulations. Some of you have come fresh from narrow jail cells. And some of you have come from areas where your quest – quest for freedom left you battered by the storms of persecution and staggered by the winds of police brutality. You have been the veterans of creative suffering. Continue to work with the faith that unearned suffering is redemptive. Go back to Mississippi, go back to Alabama, go back to South Carolina, go back to Georgia, go back to Louisiana, go back to the slums and ghettos of our northern cities, knowing that somehow this situation can and will be changed.

Let us not wallow in the valley of despair, I say to you today, my friends.

And so even though we face the difficulties of today and tomorrow, I still have a dream. It is a dream deeply rooted in the American dream.

I have a dream that one day this nation will rise up and live out the true meaning of its creed: "We hold these truths to be self-evident, that all men are created equal."

I have a dream that one day on the red hills of Georgia, the sons of former slaves and the sons of former slave owners will be able to sit down together at the table of brotherhood.

I have a dream that one day even the state of Mississippi, a state sweltering with the heat of injustice, sweltering with the heat of oppression, will be transformed into an oasis of freedom and justice.

I have a dream that my four little children will one day live in a nation where they will not be judged by the color of their skin but by the content of their character.

I have a *dream* today!

I have a dream that one day, down in Alabama, with its vicious racists, with its governor having his lips dripping with the words of "interposition" and "nullification" – one day right there in Alabama little black boys and black girls will be able to join hands with little white boys and white girls as sisters and brothers.

I have a *dream* today!

I have a dream that one day every valley shall be exalted, and every hill and mountain shall be made low, the rough places will be made plain, and the crooked places will be made straight; "and the glory of the Lord shall be revealed and all flesh shall see it together."

This is our hope, and this is the faith that I go back to the South with.

With this faith, we will be able to hew out of the mountain of despair a stone of hope. With this faith, we will be able to transform the jangling discords of our nation into a beautiful symphony of brotherhood. With this faith, we will be able to work together, to pray together, to struggle together, to go to jail together, to stand up for freedom together, knowing that we will be free one day.

And this will be the day – this will be the day when all of God's children will be able to sing with new meaning:

> *My country 'tis of thee, sweet land of liberty, of thee I sing.*
> *Land where my fathers died, land of the Pilgrim's pride,*
> *From every mountainside, let freedom ring!*

And if America is to be a great nation, this must become true.

And so let freedom ring from the prodigious hilltops of New Hampshire.

Let freedom ring from the mighty mountains of New York.

Let freedom ring from the heightening Alleghenies of Pennsylvania.

Let freedom ring from the snow-capped Rockies of Colorado.

Let freedom ring from the curvaceous slopes of California.

But not only that:

> Let freedom ring from Stone Mountain of Georgia.
> Let freedom ring from Lookout Mountain of Tennessee.
> Let freedom ring from every hill and molehill of Mississippi.
> From every mountainside, let freedom ring.

And when this happens, and when we allow freedom ring, when we let it ring from every village and every hamlet, from every state and every city, we will be able to speed up that day when *all* of God's children, black men and white men, Jews and Gentiles, Protestants and Catholics, will be able to join hands and sing in the words of the old Negro spiritual:

> *Free at last! Free at last!*
> *Thank God Almighty, we are free at last!*

This speech was delivered to a crowd of 250,000 people at the Lincoln Memorial in Washington, D.C. on 28 August 1963. Permission to reprint was granted by Writers House on behalf of the King Centre.

8

Cancel culture is for cowards

Long before he became Premier of New South Wales, Dominic Perrottet, wrote:

> *True progress demands a truly free exchange of ideas, because the best ideas are forged in the furnace of fierce disagreement – the battle of ideas, where wits are sharpened, arguments blunted, minds expanded, and gradually, truth revealed. Nothing has made this clearer to me than the responsibility of legislative decision-making. Free debate is simply indispensable to that process. But I have felt the chill setting in – the reluctance to speak out, even among colleagues, on matters of huge importance, for fear of falling foul of the PC police.[44]*

An invidious new phenomenon has invaded our world. It is called 'cancel culture'. It began in the universities and has now spread widely. It is the technique of cowards who use political influence to shut down debate.

Self-appointed, sanctimonious and frequently ignorant social justice warriors ensure that those with different views are not heard. They publicly shame and boycott individuals and companies whose opinions are, according to them, controversial, unpopular or unacceptable. Social media is used to make the impact widespread and instantaneous, and the damage permanent. Victims of these attacks are pressured into retractions and apologies reminiscent of Solzhenitsyn's Russia.

Throughout the developed world, universities are discouraging debate, banning speakers with unpopular ideas and expelling professors who do not adhere to mainstream political views. In Australia, examples include the treatment of Renee Gorman at University of Sydney, Professor

---

44   Perrottet, D. (2016)

Peter Ridd at James Cook University, and Drew Pavlou at the University of Queensland. Renee Gorman, president of Students for Liberty, was denied access to her university's facilities to show the film *The Red Pill* (Cassie Jaye, 2016) because the student union disapproved of the film. Peter Ridd, an academic at James Cook University and a passionate advocate for quality control in science, was fired after thirty years' service for publicly criticising research concerning the bleaching of corals on the Great Barrier Reef. His behaviour was described as *uncollegiate*, and the university fired him for disclosing the disciplinary action that they took. Student activist Drew Pavlou was suspended for organising a protest in support of democracy in Hong Kong. Pavlou alleged that he was suspended because 'my protests threatened a relationship with the Chinese government that was worth hundreds of millions of dollars every year, worth billions over the long-term'.[45]

Some of international examples are bizarre. J.P.E. Harper-Scott, a professor of music history and theory at the University of London, quit academia over the university's position that: 'Nineteenth-century musical works were the product of an imperial society. The classical musical canon must be decolonised'.[46] As he pointed out, the consequence

> *... could be that music departments stop teaching music by Beethoven, Wagner, and co., in the (frankly insane) belief that doing so will somehow materially improve the current living conditions for the economically, socially, sexually, religiously, or racially underprivileged.[47]*

Harry Potter author J.K. Rowling spoke out about the erosion of women's rights. She was cancelled for arguing that the acceptance of transgender people should not be to the detriment of women. She expressed concern that the legal definition of sex was being eroded and replaced with gender:

> *So I want trans women to be safe. At the same time, I do not want to make natal girls and women less safe. When you throw open the doors of bathrooms and changing*

---

45   Sammy Taylor, 60 Minutes, 9NOW, 2020.
46   https://www.spiked-online.com/2021/09/20/cancelling-classical-music/
47   https://jpehs.co.uk/why-i-left-academia/

rooms to any man who believes or feels he's a woman – and, as I have said, gender confirmation certificates may now be granted without any need for surgery or hormones – then you open the door to any and all men who wish to come inside. That is the simple truth.[48]

For these opinions, Rowling was subjected to threats of death and rape, sufficient to 'paper the house with them'.[49] The irony of such violence was lost on her detractors, who included actors who had appeared in the Harry Potter films. While her views were calmly and rationally put, those who denigrated her were very nasty people, indeed.

Cartoonists provide a valuable service. They expose our foibles to their sharp intellects, providing succinct commentary and illustration. Cartoonists have also been in the firing line of the cultural warriors. In 2016, Bill Leak incurred the wrath of the Australian Human Rights Commission when his 'What's his name then?' cartoon suggested that poor parenting was a significant factor in the incarceration of Indigenous youth. Mark Knight was pilloried in 2018 for his cartoon of tennis great Serena Williams throwing a childish tantrum after she had lost the US Open final. In 2021 Michael Leunig drew a cartoon comparing the actions of Victoria's police force, which had used rubber bullets and capsicum spray against unarmed protesters, to the well-known 'tank man' photo of a protestor standing in front of an armoured tanker at Tiananmen Square in 1989. The Age editor, Gay Alcorn, thought her readers were too precious to handle such a horrid comparison. She fired him. She replaced him with an illustrator of children's books.

Typically, the social warriors who promote the cancel culture lack a sense of humour. They are oblivious to satire. Peter Boghossian, a professor of philosophy at Portland University in the United States, had a reputation for inviting guest lecturers who would challenge his students. That earned him the disapproval of his faculty. But it was Boghossian's concern that morally fashionable journal papers were being published – no matter how absurd – that got him into real trouble. To illustrate his point, Boghossian co-published a peer-reviewed paper in

48   https://www.jkrowling.com/opinions/j-k-rowling-writes-about-her-
     reasons-for-speaking-out-on-sex-and-gender-issues/
49   https://twitter.com/jk_rowling/status/1462759297465692162

the journal *Cogent Social Sciences*, entitled 'The conceptual penis as a social construct'[50] arguing that penises were products of the human mind and responsible for climate change. That proved too much. Boghossian was harassed by both student warriors and faculty. He quit.

In the name of emotional well-being, university students are being protected from words and ideas they don't like. 'Trigger words' are identified so that unpleasant concepts are not aired, and safe spaces are provided where students can go to hide from challenges.

As Gab Saad wrote in *The Parasitic Mind: How infectious ideas are killing common sense* (2020):

> *This is precisely what plagues our universities: what were once centers of intellectual development have become retreats for the emotionally fragile. The driving motto of the university is no longer the pursuit of truth but coddling hurt feelings ... Building a society where the primary objective is to protect one's fragile self-esteem from the dangers competition will only lead to a society of weakness, entitlement, and apathy.*[51]

When theologian John Henry Newman wrote *The Idea of a University* (1853 and 1858),[52] he envisaged a community in which students were taught 'to think and to reason and to compare and to discriminate and to analyse'.[53] Newman was of the view that universities should be free of religious and ideological interference. How things have changed.

---

50   Lindsay, J and Boyle, P. (2017)
51   Saad, G. (2020) p. 27
52   Newman, J.H. (1853, 1858/1959)
53   https://www.theguardian.com/commentisfree/2010/oct/20/john-henry-newman-idea-university-soul

Jonathan Haidt (1963–)

Jonathan Haidt is an American social psychologist based at New York University's Stern School of Business. He was awarded a doctorate from the University of Pennsylvania in 1992 and taught for 16 years in the Department of Psychology at the University of Virginia.

Haidt's research examines the intuitive foundations of morality and how they vary across cultures. His goal is to help people understand each other, live and work near each other and learn from each other despite their moral differences.

Haidt has co-founded a variety of organisations and collaborations that apply moral and social psychology toward that end.

Haidt is the author of:

- *The Happiness Hypothesis: Finding modern truth in ancient wisdom* (2006)
- *The Righteous Mind: Why good people are divided by politics and religion* (2012)
- *The Coddling of the American Mind: How Good Intentions and Bad Ideas are Setting Up a Generation for Failure* (2018), co-authored with Greg Lukianoff.

He has written more than 100 academic articles.

In 2019, he was inducted into the American Academy of Arts and Sciences and was chosen by *Prospect* magazine as one of the world's top fifty thinkers. He has given four TED talks, which have been viewed more than 6 million times.

In *The Righteous Mind*, Haidt makes three telling points. Firstly, that we form our beliefs by intuition and then use reason to justify our position. That is why it is so hard to change someone's mind by reason alone. Secondly, that there is more to morality than harm and fairness. Haidt proposes a moral framework comprising:

Moral domain	Context
• Care/harm	suffering of victims
• Liberty/oppression	protection from bullies
• Fairness/cheating	proportionality
• Loyalty	to one's group (family, community, nation)
• Authority	respect for institutions (marriage, the law)
• Sanctity	decency, purity, religion

Haidt's third point is that morality binds and blinds. 'When asked to account for the development of their own religious faith and moral beliefs, conservatives underscored deep feelings about allegiance to one's group, respect for authority and purity of self, whereas liberals emphasised deep feelings about human suffering and fairness.' [54]

Haidt advised the United States Democratic Party that it needed to address the binding foundations of loyalty, authority and sanctity if it wished to appeal to a wider group of voters.

In *The Atlantic's* September 2015 cover story, *The Coddling of the American Mind*, Jonathan Haidt, writing in collaboration with Greg Lukianoff, discussed how and why 'cancel culture' is disastrous for students' education and their mental health. It is an important milestone in the recognition of a serious problem.

---

54   Haidt, J. (2012)

The Coddling of the American Mind

Greg Lukianoff and Jonathan Haidt

Something strange is happening at America's colleges and universities. A movement is arising, undirected and driven largely by students, to scrub campuses clean of words, ideas, and subjects that might cause discomfort or give offense.

Last December, Jeannie Suk wrote in an online article for *The New Yorker* about law students asking her fellow professors at Harvard not to teach rape law – or, in one case, even use the word *violate* (as in 'that violates the law') lest it cause students distress. In February, Laura Kipnis, a professor at Northwestern University, wrote an essay in *The Chronicle of Higher Education* describing a new campus politics of sexual paranoia – and was then subjected to a long investigation after students who were offended by the article and by a tweet she'd sent filed Title IX complaints against her.

Two terms have risen quickly from obscurity into common campus parlance. *Microaggressions* are small actions or word choices that seem on their face to have no malicious intent but that are thought of as a kind of violence nonetheless. For example, by some campus guidelines, it is a microaggression to ask an Asian American or Latino American "Where were you born?" because this implies that he or she is not a real American.

Trigger warnings are alerts that professors are expected to issue if something in a course might cause a strong emotional response. For example, some students have called for warnings that Chinua Achebe's *Things Fall Apart* describes racial violence and that F. Scott

Fitzgerald's *The Great Gatsby* portrays misogyny and physical abuse, so that students who have been previously victimized by racism or domestic violence can choose to avoid these works, which they believe might "trigger" a recurrence of past trauma.

Some recent campus actions border on the surreal. In April, at Brandeis University, the Asian American student association sought to raise awareness of microaggressions against Asians through an installation on the steps of an academic hall. The installation gave examples of microaggressions such as "Aren't you supposed to be good at math?" and "I'm colorblind! I don't see race." But a backlash arose among other Asian American students, who felt that the display itself was a microaggression. The association removed the installation, and its president wrote an e-mail to the entire student body apologizing to anyone who was "triggered or hurt by the content of the microaggressions."

This new climate is slowly being institutionalized and is affecting what can be said in the classroom, even as a basis for discussion. During the 2014–15 school year, for instance, the deans and department chairs at the 10 University of California system schools were presented by administrators at faculty leader-training sessions with examples of microaggressions. The list of offensive statements included: "America is the land of opportunity" and "I believe the most qualified person should get the job."

The press has typically described these developments as a resurgence of political correctness. That's partly right, although there are important differences between what's happening now and what happened in the 1980s and '90s. That movement sought to restrict speech (specifically "hate speech" aimed at marginalized groups), but it also challenged the literary, philosophical, and historical canon, seeking to widen it by including more diverse perspectives.

The current movement is largely about emotional well-being. More than the last, it presumes an extraordinary fragility of the collegiate psyche, and therefore elevates the goal of protecting students from physiological harm. The ultimate aim, it seems, is to turn campuses into "safe spaces" where young adults are shielded from words and ideas that make some uncomfortable. This new movement seeks to punish anyone who interferes with that aim, even accidentally. You might call this impulse *vindictive protectiveness.* It is creating a culture in which everyone must think twice before speaking up, lest they face charges of insensitivity, aggression, or worse.

We have been studying this development for a while now, with rising alarm.... The dangers that these trends pose to scholarship and to the quality of American universities are significant.... But..., [w]hat are the effects of this new protectiveness on the *students themselves?* Does it benefit the people it is supposed to help? What exactly are students learning when they spend four years or more in a community that polices unintentional slights, places warning labels on works of classic literature, and in many other ways conveys the sense that words can be a form of violence that require strict control by campus authorities...?

There is a common saying in education circles: Don't teach students *what* to think; teach them *how* to think. The idea goes back at least as far as Socrates. Today, what we call the Socratic method is a way of teaching that fosters critical-thinking, in part by encouraging students to question their own unexamined beliefs, as well as the received wisdom of those around them. Such questioning sometimes leads to discomfort, even to anger, on the way to understanding.

But vindictive protectiveness teaches students to think in a very different way. It prepares them poorly for professional life, which often demands intellectual engagement with people and ideas one might find uncongenial or wrong.

A campus culture devoted to policing speech and punishing speakers is likely to engender patterns of thought that are surprisingly similar to those long identified by cognitive behavioral therapists as causes of depression and anxiety. The new protectiveness may be teaching students to think pathologically...

The thinking cure

For millennia, philosophers have understood that we don't see life as it is; we see a version distorted by our hopes, fears, and other attachments.... Cognitive behavioral theory is a modern embodiment of this ancient wisdom. It is the most extensively studied nonpharmaceutical treatment of mental illness and is used widely to treat depression, anxiety disorders, eating disorders, and addictions. No other form of psychotherapy keeps working long after treatment is stopped, because it teaches thinking skills that people can continue to use.

The goal is to minimize distorted thinking and see the world more accurately. You start by learning the names of the dozen or so most common cognitive distortions (such as overgeneralizing, discounting positives, and emotional reasoning...). Each time you notice yourself falling prey to one of these distortions, you name it, describe the facts of the situation, consider alternative interpretations, and then choose an interpretation of events more in line with those facts. Your emotions follow your new interpretation.... When people improve their mental hygiene in this way..., they become less depressed, anxious, and angry.

The parallel to formal education is clear: Cognitive behavioral therapy teaches good critical-thinking skills, the sort that educators have striven for so long to impart. By almost any definition, critical-thinking requires grounding one's beliefs in evidence rather than in emotion or desire and learning how to search for and evaluate evidence that might contradict one's initial hypothesis.

But does campus life today foster critical-thinking? Or does it coax students to think in more distorted ways?

Let's look at recent trends in higher education in light of the distortions that cognitive behaviour theory identifies. We will draw the names and descriptions of these distortions from David D. Burns' popular book *Feeling Good,* as well as from the second edition of *Treatment Plans and Interventions for Depression and Anxiety Disorders,* by Robert L. Leahy, Stephen J.F. Holland, and Lata K. McGinn.

Higher Education's Embrace of "Emotional Reasoning"

…Emotional reasoning dominates many campus debates and discussions. A claim that someone's words are "offensive" is not just an expression of one's own subjective feeling of offendedness. It is, rather, a public charge that the speaker has done something objectively wrong. It is a demand that the speaker apologize or be punished by some authority for committing an offense.

There have always been some people who believe they have a right not to be offended. Yet throughout American history – from the Victorian era to the free-speech activism of the 1960s and '70s – radicals have pushed boundaries and mocked prevailing sensibilities…

Because there is a broad ban in academic circles on "blaming the victim," it is generally considered unacceptable to question the reasonableness (let alone the sincerity) of someone's emotional state, particularly if those emotions are linked to one's group identity. The thin argument, "I'm offended," becomes an unbeatable trump card.

If our universities teach students that their emotions can be used effectively as weapons… then they are teaching them a kind of hypersensitivity that will lead them into countless drawn-out conflicts that will damage their careers and friendships along with their mental health…

Mental Filtering and Disinvitation Season

As Burns defines it, *mental filtering*, is "pick[ing] out a negative detail in any situation and dwell[ing] on it exclusively, thus perceiving that the whole is negative." … When applied to campus life, mental filtering allows for simple-minded demonization.

Students and faculty in large numbers modelled this cognitive distortion during 2014's "disinvitation season". That's the time of the year when commencement speakers are announced, and when students and professors demand that some of those speakers be disinvited because of things they have said or done. According to data compiled by the

Foundation for Individual Rights in Education, since 2000, at least 240 campaigns have been launched at U.S. universities to prevent public figures from appearing at campus events: most of them have occurred since 2009...

Members of an academic community should of course be free to raise questions... But should dislike of part of a person's record disqualify her altogether from sharing her perspectives?...

If students graduate believing that they can learn nothing from people they dislike or from those with whom they disagree, we will have done them a great intellectual disservice.

What Can We Do Now?

Attempts to shield students from words, ideas, and people that might cause them emotional discomfort are bad for the students. They are bad for the workplace, which will be mired in unending litigation if student expectations of safety are carried forward. And they are bad for American democracy, which is already paralyzed by worsening partisanship.

When the ideas, values, and speech of the other side are seen not just as wrong but as wilfully aggressive toward innocent victims, it is hard to imagine the kind of mutual respect, negotiation, and compromise that are needed to make politics a positive-sum game.

Rather than trying to protect students from words and ideas that they will inevitably encounter, colleges should do all that they can to equip students to thrive in a world full of words and ideas that they cannot control. ... With this in mind, here are some steps that might help reverse the tide of bad thinking on campus ...:

Universities themselves should try to raise consciousness about the need to balance freedom of speech with the need to make all students feel welcome. Talking openly about such conflicting but important values is just the sort of challenging exercise that any diverse but tolerant community must learn to do. Restrictive speech codes should be abandoned.

Universities should also officially and strongly discourage trigger warnings. They should endorse the American Association of University Professors' report on these warnings, which notes, "The presumption that students need to be protected rather than challenged in a classroom is at once infantilizing and anti-intellectual." ...

Finally, universities should rethink the skills and values they most want to impart to their incoming students. At present, many freshman-orientation programs try to raise student sensitivity to a nearly impossible level. Teaching students to avoid giving unintentional offense is a worthy goal, especially when the students come from many different cultural backgrounds. But students should also be taught how to live in a world full of potential offenses. Why not teach incoming students how to practice cognitive behavioural therapy? Given high and rising rates of mental illness, this simple step would be among the most humane and supportive things a university could do.

[T]he outcome could pay dividends in many ways. For example, a shared vocabulary about reasoning, common distortions, and the appropriate use of evidence to draw conclusions would facilitate critical thinking and real debate. It would also tone down the perpetual state of outrage that seems to engulf some colleges these days, allowing students' minds to open more widely to new ideas and new people.

A greater commitment to formal debate on campus – and to assembling a more politically diverse faculty – would further serve that goal....

We believe that this is still – and always will be – the best attitude for American universities. Faculty, administrators, students, and the federal government all have a role to play in restoring universities to their historic mission.

The *Coddling of the American Mind* was published in *The Atlantic* in September 2015. This is an approved abridged version. Permission to reprint was granted by Jonathan Haidt and *The Atlantic*.

9

Social media engenders bigotry

John Stuart Mill made the point that ideas need to be tested in the heat of debate. Otherwise, error persists and there is no mechanism for half-truths to be modified. Beliefs that are loosely held become prejudices.

Not the violent conflict between parts of the truth, but the quiet suppression of half of it, is the formidable evil: there is always hope when people are forced to listen to both sides; it is only when they attend only to one that errors harden into prejudices, and truth itself ceases to have the effect of truth, being exaggerated into falsehood.[55]

Increasingly, I find my friends unwilling to entertain views that might challenge their preconceptions. They refuse to read alternative viewpoints, refuse to listen to alternative commentary, and they deny facts. Faced with error in their prevailing views, they will simply say 'I don't believe that'. Moreover, they often have very negative views about media publishers and broadcasters whose programs they never see nor hear.

In the 1990s, Tim Berners Lee gave us the world wide web, and telecommunications companies spent a trillion dollars wiring the world with fibre optic cable, thereby making global communications affordable. The general public's expectation was that this would make information readily available to everyone and that we could all seek the truth. It has not turned out that way.

---

55   Mill, J.S. (1859).

Social media solves the marketing problem of bringing willing buyers and sellers together very economically. If we tell our friends on social media that our daughter is engaged to be married, we will be inundated with businesses offering to sell us bridal dresses, wedding venues and gift ideas for the happy couple. Similarly, booksellers can observe what we are reading and recommend works from similar authors. This is all very useful and efficient. Businesses can target their marketing to a select group of interested buyers, and customers can be directed to useful information.

However, the effect on our understanding of political matters is less benign. Social media picks up what we have watched on YouTube and recommends more of the same. We watch that too. It observes and refines its model of what we like. It never sends us contrary views. If we like Tim Flannery or Naomi Klein or Greta Thunberg, we will never hear from Judith Curry or Roy Spencer or Richard Lindzen or Gwythian Prins.[56] Everything we watch reinforces our views. We begin to think that everyone agrees with us, and that no reasonable person could possibly think differently. Without intending to, we become bigots. Lazily. Smugly.

Yet, it is imperative if we seek truth to be prepared to listen to challenging ideas.

> *If you only read the books that everyone else is reading, you can only think what everyone else is thinking.*[57]

In addition to finding information, technology has given us the ability to publish whatever we like, unedited and at no cost. One consequence has been that on social media platforms like Facebook and Twitter, people say the most outrageous and scurrilous things, anonymously. It's not ideal. It's difficult to monitor.

This has led to another disturbing recent phenomenon. The social media platforms have taken it upon themselves to become censors. They decide who can communicate and what they may say. The platforms cancel

---

56   Prins, G. (2021).
57   Murakami, H. (2003).

or ban those with unacceptable views. For example, Twitter took down Donald Trump's account whilst he was still President of the United States, and Facebook banned articles suggesting that Covid-19 might have originated in a Wuhan laboratory. In September 2020, YouTube pulled a June 2020 interview between Peter Robinson and Scott Atlas because it violated their guidelines. The interview had focused on the safety of school reopening and the extremely low risk for children from COVID-19, including the low risk of transmission from children to adults.[58] Science-based criticism of the policies of Dr Fauci and Dr Birx had become unacceptable. Shades of 1984.

Now, as privately owned businesses, social media companies may trade with whomever they like. That is their prerogative. But as monopolies, the outcome may be the undermining of democracy. What if these social media owners were to use their commercial power for party political purposes? Imagine the effect on Australian society if only the views of one political party could be published on platforms such as Facebook, Twitter, and YouTube. Or on public broadcasters such as the ABC and SBS.

---

58   Atlas (2021), p. 316

Meg Wheatley (1944–)

Meg Wheatley is a consultant and educator in leadership and organisational theory. Her clients have ranged from the head of the United States Army to 12-year-old scouts, and from chief executives to small town ministers. She has a Master of Arts from New York University and a doctorate in administration, planning and social policy from Harvard University.

In 1992, Wheatley published *Leadership and the New Science: Discovering order in a chaotic world*. She proposed that Newtonian physics had provided the basis for organisational theory in manual work; if you wanted to get things moving, you needed to apply a little force. However, in the age of knowledge work, in order to improve productivity, people need to be inspired.

The whip is of little use if you wish to encourage architects to design buildings, journalists to write articles, or medical scientists to devise cures.

Wheatley proposed that new discoveries in biology, chaos theory and quantum physics are needed to understand how the world works. She concluded that, in the contemporary world of work, relationships are what matter. Cooperation and participation are essential, and chaos and change are the only routes to transformation.

In 1996, in *A Simpler Way*, (co-authored with Myron Kellner-Rogers), Wheatley explored how we could use our knowledge of biology, an understanding of how life works, to better organise human endeavours.

It is a practical primer for the ideas in *Leadership and the New Science*. It guided the way we organised work at Fenwick Software.

Meg Wheatley's other books include:

- *Who Do We Choose To Be? Facing reality, claiming leadership, restoring sanity (2017)*
- *So Far From Home: Lost and found in our brave new world (2012)*
- *Walk Out Walk On: A learning journey into communities daring to live the future now (co-authored with Deborah Frieze, 2011)*
- *Perseverance (2010)*
- *Finding Our Way: Leadership for an uncertain time (2005)*
- *Turning to One Another: Simple conversations to restore hope for the future (2002)*

Meg Wheatley's writing is replete with insight and understanding. Here is an example. Commenting on the GFC of 2008, she identified that organisations were not so much too big to fail but too big to manage:

> *Twentieth-century leaders built corporate empires, organizations too big to lead. Inherently unmanageable by virtue of size and complexity, inherently meaningless by virtue of work reduced to disassociated parts, these behemoths were ill prepared for this new world of rapid change and unpredictability. Faced with growing uncertainty and instability, leaders didn't understand complexity for its order-seeking capacity achieved through self-regulation. And they did not trust the people working for them.*

> *So they chose the familiar means of coercion and control, creating laws, regulations, policies, measurements. These bureaucratic means did not reduce the chaos; in fact, they created more unpredictability as unintended consequences burgeoned and worker cynicism escalated. Although the chaos was self-induced, leaders still did not know what else to do except to tighten controls, putting strangleholds on performance.[59]*

Meg Wheatley continues to write and consult. Her current project is entitled *Warriors of Human Spirit*. It is about developing leaders who recognise the harm being done to people and the planet through dominant practices that control, ignore, abuse and oppress the human spirit.

In the following excerpt from *So Far From Home,* Wheatley gives us her insights into how the trend to lazy bigotry has come about.

---

59   Wheatley, M.J. (2012) p. 119.

Excerpt from So Far from Home

Meg Wheatley

The dynamic of consumers defining themselves by personal tastes and preferences was already well in motion when the next giant influence appeared on the scene – the Internet and social networking. Almost overnight it became easy to describe who you were, what you were doing, how you were feeling, moment by moment in a never-ending stream of brief reports. Popularity became the primary driver, incredibly easy to track: how many friends, how many followers, how many re-tweets. But more important, the Net created a new arena for instant judgments. Thumbs up, thumbs down. ...

This world of thumbs going up or down, the nonstop critiquing of everything, has resulted in a culture of instant, careless, meaningless judgment. If it was only individual, it might be annoying but nothing more serious. But it exacerbates another trend began several years ago, that of losing the distinction between opinion and fact. Now we only listen to commentators whose opinions match our own, talk to people who think like us, chat online with those of the same interests. Even if we'd like to stay open and curious, we're caught in a self-sealing dynamic. We don't have time or energy to engage; it is easier to stick with those who confirm our opinions. The boundaries between us and them get stronger, and we settle into the comfort of being only with like-minded people. We become intellectually lazy, group thinkers. From here it is only one step to becoming righteous about our position, more aggressive in our stance, more fearful of those who are different. This is the road to fundamentalism – rigid views that will not be changed, only defended. And most of us are on it.

So here we have a culture of people who have been powerfully manipulated into believing they're defined by their tastes and preferences. Highly individualized identities are given unlimited, ever-present opportunities to give their opinion. Identities become rigidly defined on the basis of these judgements: You are not like me. We don't like the same things. I don't like you. I hate you. The dividing lines become very clear. My opinions continue to be strengthened by the media and commentators I listen to; they reinforce my opinions and tell me to keep thinking this way, that I am right and everyone else is either an idiot or dangerous. I soon forget, if I ever knew, that there is any other way to think about things. My judgements get strengthened every time I comment, vote, blog, post, listen to commentators. With every thumbs up or down, I feel more confirmed in my tastes. No one's challenging me; they just want to know what I like. My opinion is all that matters.

A culture of opinions moves in one direction, towards intensified fear and paranoia. Emotions can only intensify as positions solidify. What we disliked we now hate. People who disagreed with us now become enemies. Opposition now becomes evil incarnate. Anger becomes violent rage and attack. This descent into dark, violent emotions is predictable. Whenever people feel threatened at the level of identity, they draw a defensive boundary around themselves from those they think are out to destroy them. If they cracked open that boundary even for a moment by letting in a different opinion, they'd be endangering themselves.

I've encountered opposition in bringing together diverse people in conversations in a number of places where I've worked, especially when inviting people to join a community conversation or to talk about an important issue from multiple perspectives. At first I couldn't understand why my well-intentioned invitation was interpreted as a threat rather than an opportunity. Over time, I came to understand that, to them, my invitation would be a crack in their defenses, a small opening that might end up destroying their identity. And I realised they were right.

When you have a rigid identity, you can't let other people's perspectives in. Conversing with them might cause you to change your mind. Even if it is just a little change, that first one might lead to the unravelling of many other beliefs. If that happened, you could no longer identify with your culture or faith – you would no longer belong. What had appeared inviting to me was accurately perceived by them as life-threatening. People feel compelled to stay with their own kind; it's too big a risk to talk with others across the borderlines. This is the price of belonging. ...

Could we have foreseen what's emerged, this consumption-driven, opinion-centric, paranoid culture spiralling into disaster? As I have traced its emergence here, I noted how the irresistible forces of self-making, consumerism and the internet interacted and fed on one another to begin the spiral of descent. I began with the imperative of self-making, seized upon by a consumer-driven global economy. As we were cajoled, entranced, and seduced by endless opportunities to make ourselves into popular creatures, powerfully enabled by the Internet, we were negatively transformed into people of intensifying tastes and opinions. Criticism and instant judgement became the norm. Behind rigid walls of judgement and personal preferences, openness and curiosity disappeared; differences came to threaten our sense of belonging. As we became a culture of self-righteous and guarded people, did anyone care that rational thinking was disappearing, that we'd lost the distinction between facts and opinions? The clamour of opinions, voiced with ever-growing extreme rhetoric, drowned out the voice of science. Science lost its essential role of observing how the world is working and discovering solutions, not from opinions but from carefully derived evidence.

This is what's emerged, a culture of people seemingly content to defend our opinions, to deny the evidence, to ignore solutions, playing out a fate that, at its end, we most likely will rate with a thumbs down.

Excerpt from Margaret J. Wheatley, *So Far from Home: Lost and found in our brave new world*, Berrett-Koehler Publishers, Inc., 2012. p. 77-85. Permission to reprint was granted by Meg Wheatley.

10

Seeking the truth

We tend to take for granted that the truth in allegations about serious matters will be determined in the courts through assessment of evidence. Well, we used to anyway. Nowadays it is not necessarily the case.

Over the years, good practices have evolved in our legal system so that competing claims can be assessed. The courts acknowledge the unreliability of witness accounts. It is increasingly evident that our human memory can play tricks on us. We understand that individuals may put a positive slant on things and may embellish or diminish unpleasant things that have happened to them. "Recollections may vary". [60] Evidence obtained from analysis of DNA has been used to undo prior convictions based on what had then been considered reliable testimony.

Physical and documentary evidence are required to overcome the deficiencies of memory and testimony. Allegations need to be backed up with compelling facts and independent observations before they can be accepted as truth. A most important legal and common law concept is that *a person is innocent until proven guilty.*

Nowadays, three other ways of assessing the truth have come into play.

The first of these is *truth as an accusation.* Merely making an accusation is seen as sufficient to establish a person's guilt. It is enough if the

---

60 Queen Elizabeth commenting on what her son Harry and his lovely wife Meghan had told Oprah Winfrey.

accuser is credible, sincere, convincing and plausible. Politicians and commentators on social media declare 'We believe you'. The technique is not new. It was practised in Nazi Germany and communist Russia. Solzhenitsyn described how in *The Gulag Archipelago*. Such accusations can be impossible to defend. We can stand at a podium as former Australian Attorney-General Christian Porter did in 2021 and declaim that "It did not happen". But we cannot provide evidence of something that did not happen. And, in many cases, the accuser is believed, and the accused is not.

The second is *truth as emotional power*, or passion. This idea has its roots in the philosophy of Romanticism. Scepticism is replaced by enthusiasm. Accusers are believed because of the passion of their convictions, their self-certainty. Emotional accounts are more likely to be believed than those expressed stoically. No-one believed that the dingo had taken Lindy Chamberlain's baby.

The third is the idea of *truth as a narrative* of suffering. We make up our own stories. They have their own validity. Our story is believed, not because it is objectively true, but because everyone is in solidarity with us, giving us their compassion and their pity.

Peter Murphy, in his essay Kavanaugh's Trial by Ordeal concludes that:

> From time to time, it is crucial to ask whether what happened really did happen. ... In some cases, it matters greatly that our accounts of what happened to us are scrupulously accurate and can be verified with compelling evidence and reliable independent corroboration. ... In all serious practical matters, our stories have to correspond with the facts.[61]

This is all well and good. We are back to the need for evidentiary truth. In most cases that is fine. However, in sexual assault cases we have a dilemma. Sexual assault often occurs with no third-party witnesses and little physical or documentary evidence. This is especially so if the victim takes some time to make a complaint. The legal process is fraught and may prove incapable of delivering satisfactory results. It is not fit for purpose. Better solutions must be devised. But relying on truth by accusation, or

---

61 Peter Murphy, *Kavanaugh's Trial by Ordeal: Burning Truth in Effigy*, Quadrant December 2018. Essay 10

passion, or narrative, does not appear to be the way forward.

Perhaps we need to look elsewhere for solutions. Perhaps we need to find ways to diminish the incidence of sexual assault. Perhaps we need to build a society that has more respect for human dignity, more individual responsibility for our actions, and is more honest, fair, civil and compassionate in our dealings with each other. How might we do that?

In *The Better Angels of Our Nature*,[62] Stephen Pinker suggests that we may have made more progress than we realise.

---

62   Pinker, S. (2013) p. 475 - 490

Peter William Murphy (1956–)

Peter Murphy is a restless scholar and polymath.

He competed a doctorate in philosophy and politics at La Trobe University in Melbourne, under the direction of Hungarian philosopher and dissident Agnes Heller.

Murphy has held academic and administrative positions in the arts, communications and media, Hellenic language and literature, cultural studies, and in political science, at universities in Australia, New Zealand, the United States, Greece, Philippines, Denmark and England.

Peter Murphy is the author of:

- *COVID-19: Proportionality, public policy and social distancing* (2020)
- *The Political Economy of Prosperity: Successful societies and productive cultures* (2020)
- *Limited Government: The public sector in the auto-industrial age* (2019)
- *Auto-industrialism: DIY capitalism and the rise of the auto-industrial society* (2017)
- *Universities and Innovation Economies: The creative wasteland of post-industrial societies* (2015)
- *The Collective Imagination: The creative spirit of free societies* (2012)
- *Civic Justice: From ancient Greece to the modern world* (2001).

He has also co-authored four books, edited five collections and written hundreds of articles and book chapters. Murphy's books are informative and thought-provoking, well-researched and replete with interesting facts.

In *The Political Economy of Prosperity*, he advocates that students be given more time to read and for there to be less classroom teaching:

> *Contemporary societies pride themselves on education. They eagerly tell anyone who will listen how much they spend on education. Quantitative rankings of national performance often treat education resource inputs as a prime criterion of social success. Yet when we look at the results of education— that is the capacity of the country's 15-year-olds to read, write, and calculate – we find that spending per capita on education means little. There is no correlation between the levels of spending and levels of student performance. The key literacies – the ability to read and comprehend proficiently, write and reason fluently, and grasp commonplace mathematical concepts and operations – are essential to a well-functioning society. They are the foundation of the reading public. The reading public in turn is the plinth on which all other publics – be they political, media, professional, or intellectual – rest. A person`s ability to participate in public life of any kind is profoundly conditioned by their literate capacity, in particular their capacity for sola scriptura, their ability to read and understand text and judge it for themselves.*[63]

In *Universities and Innovation Economies,* he expresses his concern that our Universities are diminished because they have lost their focus.

> *Universities are defined by three great functions. One is to transmit knowledge in order to provide students with and understanding of the humanities, the sciences or the social sciences. The second function is to transmit knowledge in order to prepare students for a learned profession. The third and highest function of the university is to create knowledge. The university is thus defined by the advancement as well as the transmission of knowledge. A university that advances knowledge is different from a humanistic college or a vocational institute. The latter principally convey knowledge rather than create it. The discovery university (the type of university that advances knowledge) relies on high levels of self-education and intellectual modelling. A firmer or clearer distinction between the discovery university (on the one hand) and the humanistic college or the technological institute (on the other hand) might help to resolve some of the conundrums that we currently face as a consequence of the repeated inflation of the concept of the university. We cannot escape the simple reality, though, that a large portion of what today is called 'the university' is not a university at all.*[64]

---

63   Murphy, P. (2020-1) p. 79
64   Murphy, P. (2015) p. 5

In addition to his prolific output, Murphy has been on the Board of Self-Employed Australia (president for 2018–20), has supervised doctoral students, organised numerous academic conferences, and has been senior editor for Looksmart International. He is a regular contributor to *Quadrant* magazine.

In *Kavanaugh's Trial by Ordeal: Burning Truth in Effigy*, Peter Murphy expands on the four theories for assessing truth: truth based on evidence; truth as an accusation; truth as emotional power; and truth as a narrative. He uses the hearings into the suitability of Brett Kavanaugh to be a judge in the United States Supreme Court to illustrate how this plays out in practice.

Kavanaugh's Trial by Ordeal:
Burning truth in effigy

Peter Murphy

Trial by smear

The smearing of US Supreme Court nominee Brett Kavanaugh was hardball politics at its most disingenuous. The stakes were unambiguous. The Democrats and their supporters wanted to delay and derail his nomination. The tactic was to wait till the end of the regular nomination hearing and then leak an accusation that the judge was guilty of sexual misconduct. Base politics for sure, but Democrats had tried twice before to derail a Supreme Court nomination with confected allegations. So the ploy was not surprising. Republicans kept their nerve. They patiently navigated three weeks of brutal character assassination of a major public figure with a spotless track record. In the course of those days the Democrats attempted to turn the supplementary Senate Judiciary Committee hearing into a show trial. As that unfolded, the very nature of 'Brett Kavanaugh' changed. He was transformed from a nominee for America's highest court into a symbol of America's political division.

A part of Kavanaugh's trial by ordeal was simple political payback. Kavanaugh had worked under Ken Starr at the Office of Independent Counsel investigating legal matters related to Bill Clinton's sexual conduct. Kavanaugh's appointment as a Circuit Judge to the US Court of Appeals for the District of Columbia was blocked by Democrats for three years during the George W. Bush presidency. The Kavanaugh imbroglio, though, turned out to be much more than just opportunistic payback. The two weeks of attempted trashing of Kavanaugh's life and reputation tapped a much deeper vein in American life. A tsunami of protest, pressure, intimidation, bluster, stunts, grandstanding, demagoguery, defamation and table-thumping erupted across much of left-leaning America, leaving moderates and conservatives shocked.

At a certain point the Kavanaugh hearing stopped being about him. Instead it become a reckoning of the broader America society with itself, in particular a reckoning about the nature of truth. The Democrats put truth on trial. The result was disturbing. The Kavanaugh ordeal revealed that long-observed and once keenly-held notions of evidentiary truth have been rejected by a substantial minority of Americans, many of them in the vocal professional-managerial elite. Evidentiary truth means that an allegation or claim that we make about serious matters needs to be backed up with compelling facts and independent observations before it can be accepted.

Some of the hysteria surrounding Kavanaugh was cynical politics. If the nomination hearing could be delayed past the 2018 mid-term elections, maybe the Democrats could gain a majority in the Senate— and then vote down Kavanaugh. Or perhaps they could peel off some Republican support for the judge, forcing his withdrawal from the process, also pushing the hearing past the Congressional mid-term elections. In any event the tactics failed. Much of the credit for this was due to Senate Republican majority leader Mitch McConnell. For three years he had doggedly shepherded through a procession of conservative appointments to US federal courts. To a degree the effect of this has been to shift the balance of the courts away from their decades-long domination by liberal jurists, many of whom have displayed a strong social-engineering streak. Through an uncertain and turbulent 2016, the uncharismatic but unflappable McConnell kept his nerve. Against the odds he began to coax a historic jurisprudential shift. Few politicians ever achieve that kind of legacy.

The appointment of Kavanaugh to the Supreme Court was the climax of McConnell's judicial re-gearing. This was not because Kavanaugh was a razor-sharp conservative. He is not the kind of high-definition conservative that Robert Bork and Clarence Thomas were when they were nominated. Like Kavanaugh, Bork and Thomas were subject to aggressively-organised partisan campaigns that included false, baseless or tendentious allegations. Kavanaugh is not a Reagan conservative (or at least he wasn't before his traducing by the Democrats). Rather he is a Bush conservative. His judicial record suggests he is a little to the right of the Supreme Court's Chief Justice John Roberts but to the left of Justice Samuel Alito. In other words, Kavanaugh is not an earth-shaking nominee. And yet the earth shook. Why?

The simple explanation is fear on the part of liberal Democrats that Kavanaugh represents a shift of the Court to a more consistent five-to-four conservative majority replacing the four-to-four matrix plus the swing vote of the retiring Supreme Court judge Anthony Kennedy. Kennedy was a Reagan-era appointment. He was a mild libertarian whose judgments at different times concurred with the Left and the Right. His swing character is evident from his judicial opinions. At various times, he opined that there was no legal limit on detaining illegal immigrants and no automatic deportation for aliens convicted of crimes. Imprisoned terrorists had *habeas* rights. Obamacare was not allowable under the Commerce Clause of the constitution but was valid as a tax. Obamacare's individual mandate was unconstitutional. States cannot ban cigarette ads near schools. Corporate political spending is free speech. Flag burning can't be outlawed. There is a presumption in favour of state rights. Admissions preferences are unconstitutional racial balancing. School vouchers are generally constitutional. The Clean Water Act is restricted to navigable waters. States can request that the Environmental Protection Agency regulate greenhouse gases. The court's *Roe* ruling definitively resolved the contentious abortion law issue. States are permitted to outlaw late termination of pregnancy. There is a constitutional right to gay marriage. Sociological analysis is insufficient to demonstrate gender bias. And so on. Something for the Left and something for the Right.

Liberals fear the loss of Kennedy's swing vote, which favoured a number of their pet moral causes. Kavanaugh's record does suggest a legal outlook less defined by libertarian moral issues. He appears sympathetic to national security surveillance, open to social security privatisation, inclined to a modestly more strict interpretation of immigration rights, disinclined to gun control and supportive of taxpayer subsidies for religious schools. In other words, Kavanaugh is a pretty conventional

Bush-era conservative. That means he is an anathema to liberals.

The fears of liberals focus particularly on the fate of *Roe v Wade*. The Supreme Court's 1973 ruling had the effect of nationalising abortion law in the United States. To a distant observer, the hysteria of American liberals about *Roe* is odd. Even if a hypothetical conservative majority on the Court decided that *Roe* was no longer settled law, all that would mean is that abortion law would go back to being a state government responsibility. Some states would opt for tougher limits on abortion; others would liberalise the rules. Overall little net change would occur. However, remember that the battle over the composition of the Supreme Court is as much about symbolism as it is about the nature of the law.

"Kavanaugh" is now and forever no longer a flesh and blood judge. He has turned into a symbol. To American liberals he signifies their deepest suspicions and anxieties. Among conservatives and moderates "Kavanaugh" stands for "abuse of due process by liberals". In a more general sense, he symbolises the face-off between social hysteria and calm. Deeper still, the battle over his nomination has touched a raw nerve in American society. In doing so it raised profound questions about the nature of truth. It did this in a way that called upon everyday Americans to ask themselves: How would I behave in this situation? What if I was the accused or the accuser? What would I regard as sufficient to establish the truth of the matter? Americans watching the blanket coverage of the Senate hearings and related goings-on could not but ask themselves some weighty questions about the nature of truth. A society rarely asks itself "What is truth?" When it does, the question points to an underlying schism in society.

Jacobin accusation

In the Kavanaugh hearings, four theories of truth were presented: truth based on evidence, truth as accusation, truth as emotional power, and truth as a narrative of suffering. Each theory had its protagonists. These are not classroom theories. They are theories that are operative in human behaviour.

Throughout the Kavanaugh controversy most Republicans repeatedly and calmly insisted that an allegation of misconduct had to be corroborated and supported by evidence. A person, including a person of high public standing, is innocent until proven guilty, even in the mischievous court of public opinion. Innocence is assumed and any guilt has to be demonstrated. This is based on an evidentiary theory of truth. It requires the marshalling of evidence and a rational demonstration that the available evidence supports or doesn't support a conclusion of guilt. What is striking about the Kavanaugh nomination is how his political opponents rejected the notion that facts are crucial in determining the truth of a claim. They relied instead on not one but three other entirely different theories of truth.

The first of these alternative theories is the idea that truth is a matter of accusation. That theory was pushed by Democratic activists and operatives. According to this idea an accusation of a certain type does not need to be proved but is inherently true. This may sound strange to anyone brought up in the tradition of Anglo-American law. But the equation of accusation and truth has many modern expressions. These range from moral panics to despotic politics. Of the latter, some of the better-known examples are the Jacobins in the French Revolution and the Stalinists in the Soviet Union. In circumstances where political fright or moral scare dominates the social atmosphere, merely making an accusation is sufficient to establish a person's guilt.

In Kavanaugh's case the accusation was made by a Californian academic, Christine Blasey Ford. She alleged that when Kavanaugh was a seventeen-year-old he had attempted to rape her. Armed with the accusation, Democrats tried to hijack the Senate process to confirm Kavanaugh's nomination. Their clear intent was to turn the process into a show trial. However, they weren't entirely successful. They did insist on the classic show-trial presumption that the accused is guilty. Kavanaugh was not only guilty till proven innocent, but nothing could prove his innocence. However, Republicans pushed back. They quietly but firmly insisted that the accusation made by Blasey Ford had to be supported by evidence.

When we ask for evidence, we imply that an allegation needs

substantiation, corroboration and confirmation. That is, it must be supported. If not, then it's not true. Initially Democrats promised corroboration and confirmation. But the evidence provided didn't stand up to scrutiny. Three persons were supposed to have either witnessed the alleged event or been at the party where the attempted rape was supposed to have occurred. All denied having been at the party or having witnessed anything of the kind. One of the witnesses who rejected the claim was a long-time female friend of the accuser.

Other evidence offered was of a pseudo-scientific kind. To prove her bona fides, Blasey Ford took a polygraph test. Polygraphs are junk science. They don't do what they claim – namely, demonstrate that a person is being truthful. The physiological reactions they measure can be equally produced by a person telling the truth, telling a lie or believing honestly in a falsehood. In any event "telling the truth" (as one believes it to be) is not the same as establishing "the truth of what happened".

Much of what the Democrats presented had nothing to do with objective truth. It was not a substantiation that "this is what happened". Rather it was a claim of subjective truth. The contention was that the accuser was an authentic person. She was telling the truth as she saw it. A number of Republican commentators also took this view, arguing that Blasey Ford presented as a "credible" person. They thought she appeared to be sincere, convincing, plausible and believable.

After the Blasey Ford allegation was made public, the Democrats and their many vocal supporters took a series of steps. These were designed to direct public opinion away from the theory that truth is something that is tested by offering evidence and evaluating that evidence. The first step was to introduce the idea that the truth of a certain privileged kind of allegation does not require evidence. Rather, an accusation of this type is sufficient and valid in itself. To underscore the point, in the two weeks of high national melodrama, the Blasey Ford allegation was followed by a series of other, ever more preposterous accusations. The second step was to insist that the accuser's "credibility" was key to the outcome of the hearing. This idea was retailed by Democrats and some Republicans alike.

Romantic authenticity

Like the show-trial theory of truth that equates truth with accusation, the equating of truth with authenticity has deep historical roots. These lie in Romanticism, the literary and political movement that emerged in Europe in the late eighteenth century. Romanticism coined the idea of an "authentic" person. The Romantic theory of truth says that an accusation can be sufficient and valid in itself if the accuser is authentic or "believable". If you are a certain kind of accuser, then your accusation should be "believed". The accuser who needs to be "believed" is one who is "credible", "sincere" and "authentic". The measure of sincerity is strong emotion. The accuser who states their accusation with emotional intensity is one who has a strong claim to be believed.

The Jacobins in the French Revolution fashioned the idea that nothing more than an accusation was needed to have someone imprisoned or sent to the guillotine. The Romantic model of truth held that emotional intensity is sufficient to establish that a person is "telling the truth". If an accuser emotes with conviction, a truth claim thereby acquires credibility. Truth in effect rests on the emphatic emotion of the accuser. When faced with an accuser who is "credible" or "believable", the seeming principal way out for the accused under these circumstances is to show that the accuser is a liar. But in the Kavanaugh case this placed Republicans between the horns of a dilemma. For how does someone show that a "believable" person is lying when there is almost no evidence for or against the accusation, and many people are arguing that the accusation is valid in itself or made valid by virtue of the authenticity of the accuser?

One of the things this points to is that truthfulness (that is, not lying) is an over-rated indicator of truth. Though an admirable human trait, truthfulness is not the same as truth. Truth is a deeper, more strenuous quality than truthfulness, even though the two are often confused.

To illustrate the point, let's ask the question: Did Blasey Ford lie? At least two of the claims she testified to were untrue. She does not have a fear of flying, nor is she claustrophobic. These were the kinds of fears that could have been the result of a teenage trauma. So did she lie? Or were these claims part of a consoling story about an event the memory of which was added to, subtracted from, compounded, embossed, embroidered or embellished over the years? We'll never know. What we do know is that human memory is not especially reliable. Nor is uncorroborated eyewitness testimony. The number of wrongful convictions based on eyewitness testimony that much later have been overturned by DNA evidence is striking. Accounts provided by human beings are fallible. Humans don't need to lie in order to get things wrong. Falsehood is not just intentional deception. People believe all sorts of things that are simply wrong.

At the same time, out of necessity, we have to trust others even though their view of things may be unreliable. A society of systemic suspicion is just as destructive as a society of liars. This is also why we have public methods of testing beliefs. We accept a vast amount of the accounts that are provided by our fellows. But we reserve the right to test beliefs if we think that something important might not have been accurately described. This is time-consuming, which is why we don't do it routinely. An all-consuming scepticism is a form of madness. This is also why legal justice is an inherently expensive business. Gathering evidence and cross-referencing accounts is laborious. So is the meta-testing of that evidence for reliability. So also is the process of examining the underlying claims to see if they are consistent, plausible, and whether they fit the facts.

We do something much less rigorous yet roughly the same in the court of public opinion. Or at least we do so in societies that ask sceptical questions and value finding evidence for and against claims. The historic effect of Romanticism has been to partially replace that scepticism with enthusiasm. Romantic culture places emphasis on passionate beliefs. It invites us to display passionate convictions. By this measure, truth is a quality that is rooted in self-certainty. If I am absolutely convinced that "this happened to me", and I express this self-certainty in a forceful manner, then my belief is "true". This theory has had a big effect on modern societies. Our contemporaries, including juries, are more disposed to believe accounts that are expressed with emotional power. Persons who express things stoically, in a matter-of-fact manner, are less likely to be believed.

That is what 250 years of Romanticism has done to our concept of truth. The subjective and expressive side of things increasingly has replaced the objective and factual. This is why the turning point in the Kavanaugh hearing occurred when Kavanaugh got angry. To that point Blasey Ford was "credible". Even many Republican commentators thought so. The White House counsel Don McGahn saved the Kavanaugh nomination when he advised Kavanaugh to come out fighting. Kavanaugh did so, impressively. What people wanted to hear was not the facts but Kavanaugh's deep sense of outrage at being accused of a horrible act he did not commit. In short, he turned the Romantic knife-edge of the larger culture against itself. He waged war against emotion and authenticity with emotion and authenticity. He won the day.

This did not please everyone. In a show trial, if individuals defend themselves, that defence is proof of their guilt or their wicked nature. So it was in Kavanaugh's case. When he defended himself vigorously in the spirit of Romantic emotivism, Kavanaugh's detractors then argued he did not have the right "judicial temperament" and so was not qualified for office. Coming from the Romantic Left, which continually engages in high-pitched screeching and emotive demonisation, that was laughable.

Yet while one can match Romantic pique with Romantic pique, the battle of emotions still leaves unanswered the question of the truth of the matter. For strength of emotion is not a criterion of truth. It is not even a sure indicator of honesty or truthfulness even if it is now often taken for such. The underlying culture of authenticity that equates truthfulness and truth is deeply flawed. It contends that it is not facts that establish truth or reality but rather authentic personalities. These personalities are "true" because they present matters with passionate conviction. Intensity signals to an audience that a speaker is "real" or "genuine". This is a trick of rhetoric, yet it is one that is deeply ingrained in modern culture. Unfortunately, this trick is also deeply misleading. For human beings often lie and these lies are difficult to detect. Humans also regularly convince themselves that fiction is fact.

Authenticity is a cue. It is not only liars or dissemblers who use the cue. So do the self-deceived, the delusional and the sophistic. Self-delusion is even more difficult to detect than lies are. All lie-detecting techniques— such as reading "body language" or conducting polygraph tests—are pseudoscientific nonsense. They assume that the body can't lie. So when you cross your arms you are being defensive (and not just huddling your body against the cold). You inadvertently reveal what your words are hiding. Except that you may be completely convinced of what you are saying—and not hiding anything at all even though what you are saying is inaccurate, unreliable, wrong or just plain ridiculous. People believe the silliest of things. Our bodies are no less capable of conveying false conviction, deception and self-deception than our speech is.

Human beings are double beings. This condition is distinct from the rest of creation. The human "I" is different from the human "me". How the "I" represents the "me" to others is variable. This is not just a question of whether we are truthful or whether we lie. For there are many shades of grey. We all communicate using half-truths, omissions and exaggerations. Everyday politics and social life are inconceivable without these. The accounts of what we witness are frequently unreliable, as are the accounts of our own lives. As a rule, memoirs and autobiographies are not very trustworthy or even very revealing. The number of persons who have been falsely imprisoned because of mistaken eyewitness testimony should give us pause for thought. Even so, we can believe deeply and adamantly—passionately—in the accounts that we provide. "This," emphatically, "is what happened." Yet often it didn't happen that way. In fact, it could not have happened that way.

Try remembering some significant event from the distant past. Then compare it with the documentary evidence from that time. Yes, you misremembered it, invented it or revised it. We all do that. One of the reasons the human species has been such an evolutionary success (relatively speaking) is that it has learnt to "objectivate". That is, it has learnt to store knowledge in external documents rather than in the human memory. It has also learnt to be "objective" in the sense of testing human belief against other people's accounts, physical evidence and documentary evidence. And also by testing the evidence. This is necessary because what we observe and what we remember is very selective (our mind has to economise) and when we recall things our mind just fills in the details (inaccurately).

There is also the propensity of the human imagination to compress images of events and experiences into imaginative fictions. Dreams are the universal example of this. These fictions may have their own kind of truth. This is the sort of truth, for example, that we find in stories. But it is not factual truth; creative perhaps, but not objective. In some cases, the fiction is simply fantasy. It's a concoction of the way we wish things were. Sometimes it's consolation or explanation or compensation for painful things that happen to us. Sometimes these fictions prove to be an interesting way of viewing the world. But they are not very useful in telling us what happened at a specific time and place to this person or that person. For that we need physical evidence, documentary evidence and corroboration from multiple other people's accounts.

Postmodern narrative

A crucial aspect of what we call truth relies on objectivity. It requires impartial, independent and detached verification. We have to test claims about "what happened" with evidence that is separate from our personal recollection and observation. For this we need facts. This might seem a straightforward proposition. Yet we live in a society that's been semi-Romanticised. This has caused objectivity to be partly replaced by emotivism. And over the top of emotivism has been spread yet another distorting layer. This is the idea of truth as a narrative of suffering.

Like emotivism, this idea also has roots in modern Romantic culture, specifically in the elevation of the literary imagination as a source of cultural truth. In the past half-century this thread has gained greater traction with the rise of postmodernism. It is difficult to overestimate how much the seeming obscurities of postmodern literary theory have quietly entered into the mainstream of social thinking. In part this was a function of the rise of the mass university which, often unconsciously, has imparted the pieties of postmodernism to the broader culture. Even many of the most prosaic and scientific disciplines in the universities have casually picked up the core nostrums of postmodern thinking.

One of the key tenets of postmodernism is that truth is a narrative. Richard Rorty, the leading American postmodernist, expressed this in varying ways. He depicted truth as a function of metaphoric description, poetic contingency, transient theory and idiosyncratic storytelling. Traditionally understood, truth is a mirror or re-presentation of reality. It supposes that we can distinguish between reality and our interpretation of reality. It focuses on *finding* the truth. Postmodernism, Rorty argued, focuses on *making* the truth. It replaces evidentiary truth with narrative meaning. The discovery of facts is replaced by evocative storytelling in particular about cruel and humiliating acts. Truth becomes a specific way that we interpret and narrate the world. This narration has no connection with reality. It is not a mirror of reality. It doesn't claim to correspond with reality. Rather it is a function of the vocabularies we use. Those vocabularies are contingent. They change. People who use old vocabularies are justly liable to be humiliated by those who use the latest vocabularies. All vocabularies are temporary.

Postmodernism derives from the views of the nineteenth-century German philosopher Friedrich Nietzsche. In the second half of the twentieth century Nietzsche's outlook became as influential on the political Left as Marx's had been in the first half of the twentieth century. For Nietzsche, truth was a mobile army of metaphors, metonymies and anthropomorphisms. These are human relations that have been "poetically and rhetorically intensified, transferred, and embellished". Human relations "rhetorically intensified" perfectly describes postmodern truth. Under its wing, Rorty mused, metaphors of self-creation ("idiosyncratic narratives") replace traditional realist ideas of truth, rationality and moral obligation. Seeing ourselves against the backdrop of something "out there" is replaced by seeing ourselves "in our own terms". Self-creation replaces discovery. In self-creation we describe a "past that the past did not know". What matters are the self-overcoming stories we tell. There is no standpoint outside of these from which we can judge these narratives. They don't have to match facts. The difference between perversity and genius, Rorty suggested, is that in the case of genius other people adopt the metaphors that we use to describe our obsessions. That way private obsession intertwines with public need.

Rorty first came to public prominence in 1980 when he published *Philosophy and the Mirror of Nature*, where he argued for a new kind of theory of theories. Rorty's view was anchored in a still more famous book, Thomas Kuhn's *The Structure of Scientific Revolutions*, which appeared in 1962. Kuhn argued that science advances by moving from one conceptual paradigm or framework to another. Kuhn's thesis was incredibly influential in universities for decades. It became an intellectual cliché. Rorty carried it (and a number of associated ideas) a couple of steps further. In doing so he sought to sever the traditional relationship between theories and the world.

Theories, Rorty thought, are essentially imaginative stories. Conversely, reality is not independent of theories. To the extent that they exist, hard facts are just narrated descriptions of experiences. Such experiences are often cruel, brutal, painful and humiliating. We should not ask questions about the relation between such experiences and a purportedly independent reality because, Rorty argued, there is no reality independent of theory or story. Our descriptions are essentially extensions of the stories we tell. Those stories or theories have no reference to the real world. They refer not to an objective reality but rather to "what we believe now". Consequently, we cannot expect theory-stories to fit the facts. If our stories define reality, then no facts about that reality can prove or disprove our stories. Facts are experiences and if our story matches our experience, it is true. The corollary of this is that truth makes no sense except as an "intra-theoretic notion", that is as part of a web of theory-stories.

The view that narratives replace facts is commonplace in contemporary media culture and the universities. Many news outlets now retail narratives rather than facts. Events are reported by being inserted into the latest fashionable narrative line. The same is true of universities. It's easy to hoax academic journals in the social sciences and humanities because so many articles in those journals today are indistinguishable from fictions. Their point is not to discover something significant about the way the world works but rather to tell a story that, as long as it follows a couple of basic precepts, is immune from criticism. The most basic precept is that the author must invoke a story-line that is dark in nature. I mean this in the sense that the story must have as its pivot or spine a description of trauma, oppression or suffering. It is not enough, as in the Romantic account of truth, that a person states a claim with "conviction". Rather, in the postmodern version, the person's story must be of the kind that invites "solidarity".

A successful hardworking white prep-school boy from an affluent conservative Maryland suburb, like Kavanaugh, does not merit and cannot elicit such solidarity. The opposite applies to a successful prep-educated white female academic from an affluent hyper-liberal California suburb who works in a university psychology department that focuses on trauma, suffering and victim narratives. Blasey Ford's Palo Alto University program says that it teaches its students to be "science minded while appreciating the larger role of psychology in alleviating suffering in the world". It offsets traditional "evidence-based clinical models" with its mission to produce "culturally competent clinical psychologists". The postmodern subsuming of "evidence" by "cultural competence" is deeply embedded in its intellectual agenda.

In Palo Alto the Anglo-American tradition of scientific and professional scepticism finds itself overtaken by claims of narrative-driven "cultural competence". Science is outweighed by stories of suffering. The initiators of the Kavanaugh drama sought to replicate this on a national stage. Defenders of the conservative prep-school boy and the liberal prep-school girl confronted each other with different standards of truth. For Kavanaugh supporters, truth is traditional evidentiary truth. For Blasey Ford defenders, truth is the truth of a narrative that tells a story of suffering. Believe the accuser, they insist. Nothing more is required. No evidence is needed. The narrative alone is sufficient. It is self-validating. It has no reference to anything outside of itself except other narratives of suffering and cruelty.

Rorty began his intellectual career in postmodernism arguing that we are in no position to offer reasons for choosing one set of descriptions over another. Then he claimed that "new" narratives were better than "old" narratives, but added that narratives which expose pain, suffering and cruelty have a special status. In the past four decades as postmodern culture has spread, society has been engulfed by a roiling procession of narrative lines, each more bleak than the previous ones. These tell tales of unhappiness, discomfort, insecurity, bleakness, disappointment, thwarted aspiration, and on and on. Each outbids the other to be dark and forbidding.

In 1985 Rorty published an essay titled "Solidarity or Objectivity?" In it lie the intellectual roots of the rage against Kavanaugh. Rorty argued that the old cognitive virtue of objectivity had to be replaced by the moral imperative of solidarity. This is exactly what the American political Left insisted throughout the dispute over Kavanaugh. Empathy with claims of assault over-rules any objective evaluation of whether an assault has taken place. This is the core of the outlook of American postmodernism. It is an attitude that emerged in the universities in the 1980s and has now propagated itself widely outside the universities. It assumes that warm sympathy outweighs cold detachment. Accordingly, stoic impassivity is a sign of viciousness, and scepticism is a form of heartless depravity. Empathic belief is all-important. One is obliged to "believe the victim" without any evidence or verification. It is not necessary to ask if an accusation is true or false, because objectivity is no longer a relevant criterion. Solidarity, compassion and pity have replaced it.

Reality check

Facts, though, are stubborn things. They are not so easy to brush away. They defy waves of anxiety and attacks of panic. They soldier on stoically, through torrents of rage and anger, in order to make their point. Their role is pivotal, not least when allegations are made about supposed criminal conduct.

Modern liberal societies are founded on two precepts. These are the basis of civil society. One is "minimise violence". The other is "minimise fraud". In cases of alleged rape, the two have a complex relationship. A mark of a good society is that sexual violence is reduced to close to zero but that in punishing violators no one is wrongly accused or convicted. These dual imperatives often have a tense relationship. On the one hand sexual assault is often difficult to prove as it occurs principally in private between two parties known to each other. Relatively few reported rape cases proceed to court. As with physical assault generally, there is a fairly low level of reporting of sexual assaults. On the other hand, the incidence of false reporting and baseless allegations of rape is high compared with other serious crimes such as murder.

The profound tension between "overcoming force" and "overcoming fraud" forms the background not just of the Kavanaugh hearing but of the entire contemporary social response to rape. This is a volatile, even explosive background. Decent persons find themselves torn between empathy with those reporting an assault and a scepticism that asks for objective proof of an assault and not just an allegation. This is almost an impossible dilemma. It throws any civil society debating the question into tortured knots.

To be detached when weighing an allegation of sexual assault is difficult. This is because in almost all cases rape is the act of a man assaulting a woman. The act brutally evokes that impossibly complex question: What is the proper relationship. between the sexes? The sensitivities, subtleties and ambiguities of the sometimes unfathomable relationship between men and women make sexual assault a topic that in so many ways resists analytic scrutiny. Yet needs must. For human beings have a strong propensity to make things up—both innocently and maliciously. This is not just that some of them, men and women, are liars. They are also poor witnesses with faulty memories. Some are fantasists and fabulists. Their imagination over-determines reality. Then there are those who tell themselves stories they find satisfying or consoling but that have no correlation with reality.

Postmodern culture exacerbates this normal human proclivity. It defines us as story-tellers. It says that these stories can't be rationally scrutinised and that they are indifferent to reality. They have no objective correlative. As Rorty put it, they are just part of a web of belief. They don't refer to reality but rather to other stories. What is important are the words we use. These words change over time. We acquire new—and invariably bleaker ways—of talking about ourselves. These narratives have no firm or mimetic connection with the world.

But we all need a reality check. From time to time, it is crucial to ask whether what happened really did happen. None of us are very accurate when we report what happened to us—irrespective of whether the event was in the distant past or just recently. We make up details and we omit others. Mostly we get by when we do this, and no harm occurs. But in some cases, it matters greatly that our accounts of what happened to us are scrupulously accurate and can be verified with compelling evidence and reliable independent corroboration. In the handful of things that really matter in life, we need to be able to provide reasons why someone else should believe us. In all serious practical matters, our stories have to correspond with the facts.

Kavanaugh's Trial by Ordeal was published in *Quadrant*, December 2018, vol. LXII, no. 552. Permission to reprint was granted by Peter Murphy and *Quadrant*.

Conclusion

Striving to build a better society

It is noteworthy that the brilliant intellects who drafted the American Constitution and the Declaration of Independence asserted that man had the right to the pursuit of happiness, not the right to be happy. It leaves open how individuals might define their happiness and makes it clear that it is not someone else's responsibility.

A good society will bring out the best in its people. It will enable them to flourish; to develop their talents to the fullest; to develop their character and their ability to reason; to provide opportunities for them to exercise their talents and abilities; and to increase their human sensibility and their ability and willingness to relate positively to others. Happiness will come from a life well lived; from fulfilling our potential as human beings; from a working life that is useful to ourselves and our fellow humans. Happiness is the intellectual activity of the morally serious and virtuous person.

How shall we go about creating the environment in which citizens might flourish? Firstly, our cultural norms and laws need to encourage the virtues we wish to instil – prudence, justice, fortitude, love, thrift, reliability, trustworthiness, courage, temperance, civility, generosity, hospitality, faith, hope, charity, diligence, industriousness, fairness, honour and so on.

Secondly, we need to provide our citizens, especially the young, with formal education in mathematics, science, music, the arts and humanities. Also, we need to pay attention to their physical education, and the lessons that can be learnt from sporting activities and from playing in teams.

We need to introduce young people to our heritage: to the great thinkers, writers and artists of the past. We want them to be proud of the civilisation to which they belong. We want our future decision makers to be knowledgeable.

This can only ever be a start. We need to whet the appetites of our young citizens for a lifelong love of learning. We need to provide opportunities through sporting facilities, art galleries and concert halls, libraries and universities, and access to the internet, to facilitate this.

There is so much to learn that any one person will acquire only a fraction of the available knowledge. Therefore, curricula need to be diverse and not limited by dogma nor arbitrary restrictions. The corollary is that we need to be wary of a state-controlled education system:

> *A general State education is a mere contrivance for moulding people to be exactly like one another; and as the mould in which it casts them is that which pleases the predominant power in the government, whether this be a monarch, a priesthood, an aristocracy, or the majority of the existing generation, in proportion as it is efficient and successful, it establishes a despotism over the mind, leading by natural tendency to one over the body. An education established and controlled by the State, should only exist, if it exists at all, as one among many competing experiments, carried on for the purpose of example and stimulus, to keep the others up to a certain standard of excellence.[65]*

Thirdly, everyone needs to learn how to cooperate productively and creatively with others, always doing the best they can with their talents. We need to pass on practical wisdom about work and how to live our lives well. Primarily, this needs to be done by example – within the family and through mentoring and apprenticeships. Much more can be learnt this way than in the classroom, for the student has a practical involvement in the subject matter and a purpose for learning.

> *For the things we have to learn before we can do them, we learn by doing them, e.g. men become builders by building and lyre players by playing the lyre; so too we become just by doing just acts, temperate by doing temperate acts, brave by doing brave acts.[66]*

---

65   Mill, J.S. (1859).
66   Aristotle (350 BCE)

Further, our young citizens need to gain valuable experiences from their participation in voluntary organisations, performing tasks outside their normal routine, acting together with people who are neither family nor work colleagues, exercising judgement and becoming familiar with the concerns of others.

Finally, our organisations need to provide our citizens with the environment in which they might practise and gain experience in whatever they wish to do; to be given the freedom to experiment, to test new ideas and new ways of doing things; and to be able to make mistakes and to learn from them without the fear of carping criticism. Their supervisors, mentors and peers need to help when they are struggling and to use judgement to ensure that mistakes are not catastrophic.

At Fenwick Software, we summarise these values and attitudes in our employment agreement:

> *You will be granted an appropriate degree of autonomy and will be responsible for your own actions. You will have opportunities to learn and to grow and to assume more and more responsibility. You will commit yourself diligently to apply all your skills and efforts to this end. Your primary responsibility is to provide value for your clients.*

Colleagues have argued with me that ours is a special case – that we have carefully selected educated, articulate, caring young people to work with. Can our experiences be generalised? I think they can.

The inalienable rights to life, liberty and the pursuit of happiness are what distinguishes humans from other creatures. These are qualities like the ability to think rationally, to empathise with others, to trust strangers, to improve ourselves and our environment by our own actions; to leave the world a better place than we found it. This is the quality of human dignity. Such dignity is inherent in everyone.

The philosophers of the Enlightenment told us that liberty works and that prosperity flows from it. Two hundred years of history has shown us that this is true – that it works in practice. Moreover, it applies, not just in the Anglosphere or in the developed world. The concepts are valid universally.

Societies which have embraced liberal democratic principles – individual rights, private property, the rule of law, and representative government – have thrived. Now everyone can live happy, prosperous and meaningful lives if they and their leaders choose to build their societies on these principles.

We should be proud of our heritage, confident in our achievements, and prepared to fight against forces that might unwittingly seek to destroy them. We are the fortunate. Let's keep it that way.

Appendices

I

One hundred years of growth worldwide

Our World in Data is a treasure trove of information on poverty, disease, hunger, climate change, war, existential risks, and inequality. It has been built by Max Rosser and his team in collaboration with the University of Oxford. On their website you will be able to find charts of GDP per capita reconstructed over time for individual countries and for the entire world.[67]

The immediate reports of disastrous events that we hear on the nightly news or read in the daily papers tend to distort our views. We gain a better understanding of the world by examining trends.

The following graphs illustrate the increasing affluence of the citizens of most countries over the past hundred years, and for some, more particularly over the past thirty. For each region, I have chosen a representative sample. Observe the contrasts: China and Taiwan; North and South Korea; Estonia and Ukraine; Botswana and Zimbabwe. Note which countries are not on the upward trend. Think about the reasons why Syria and Venezuela are in decline.

You can access the data at www.ourworldindata.org and create your own versions or find information about other countries and other times. Enjoy.

---

67   www.ourworldindata.org

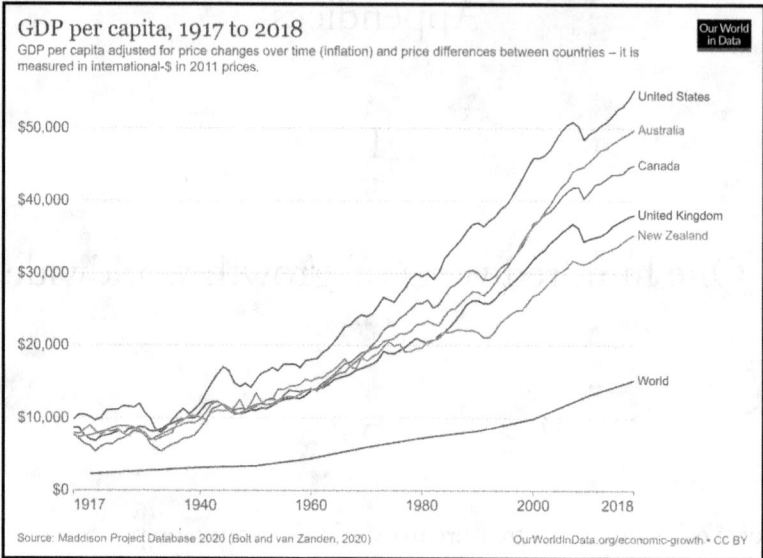

Fig. 1 The Anglosphere

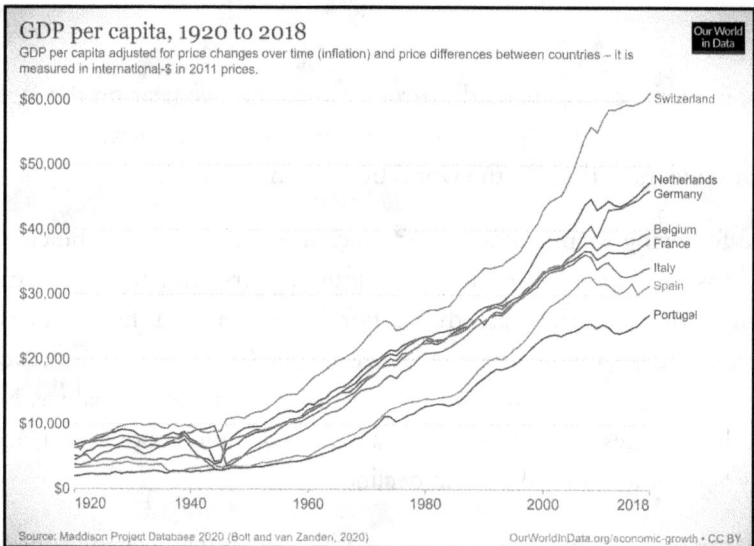

Fig. 2 Western Europe

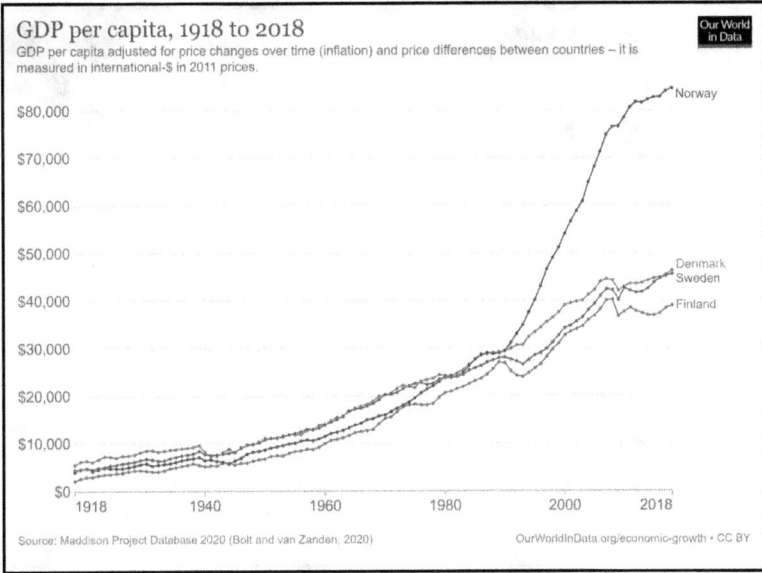

Fig 3   Scandinavia & Finland

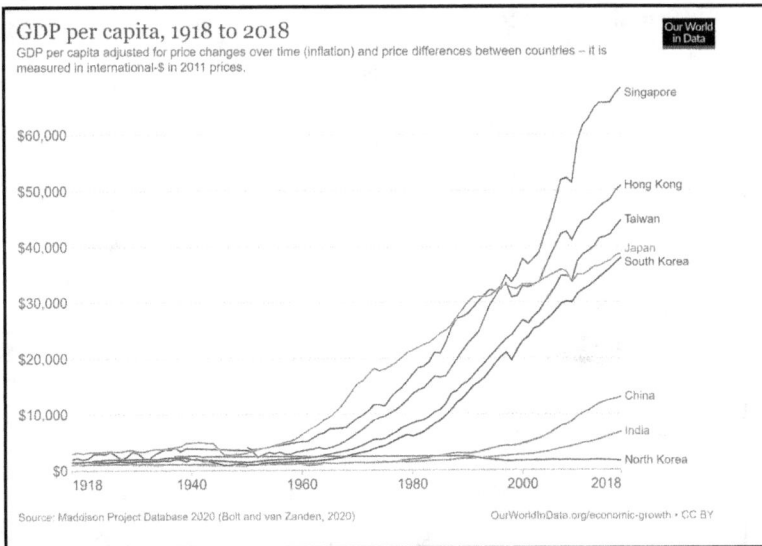

Fig. 4   Asia

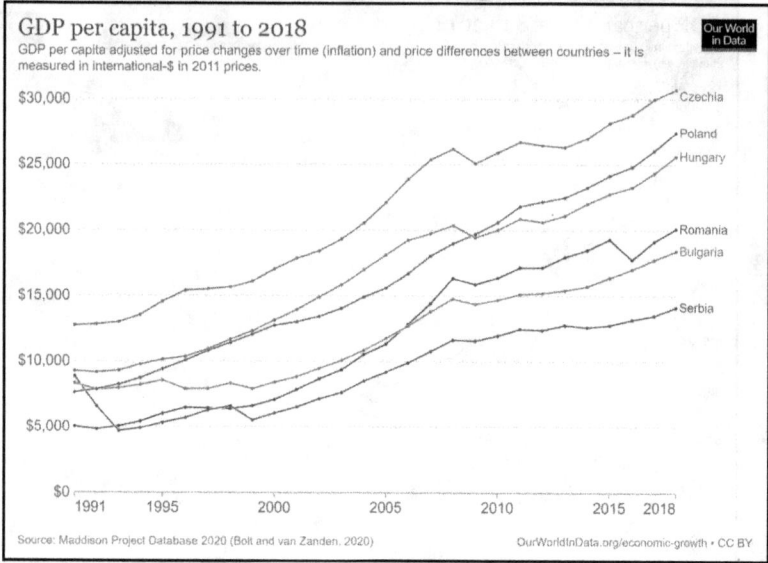

GDP per capita, 1991 to 2018
GDP per capita adjusted for price changes over time (inflation) and price differences between countries – it is measured in international-$ in 2011 prices.

Source: Maddison Project Database 2020 (Bolt and van Zanden, 2020)   OurWorldInData.org/economic-growth • CC BY

Fig. 5   Eastern Europe

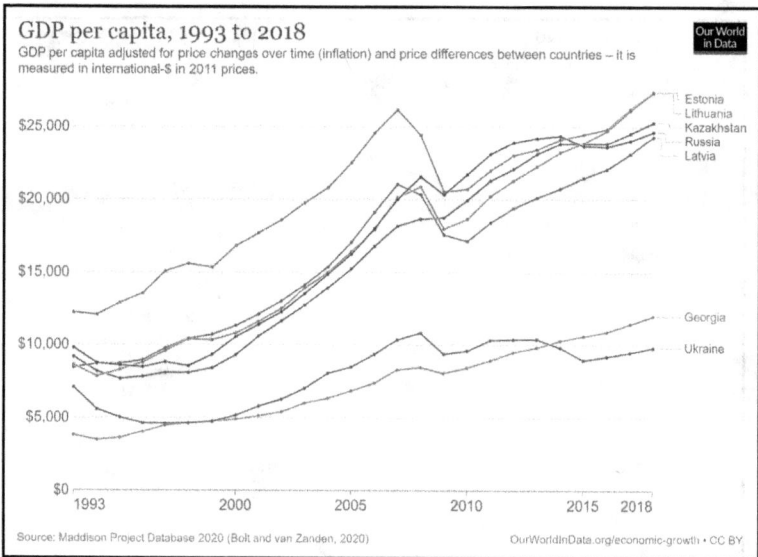

GDP per capita, 1993 to 2018
GDP per capita adjusted for price changes over time (inflation) and price differences between countries – it is measured in international-$ in 2011 prices.

Source: Maddison Project Database 2020 (Bolt and van Zanden, 2020)   OurWorldInData.org/economic-growth • CC BY

Fig. 6   The Former USSR

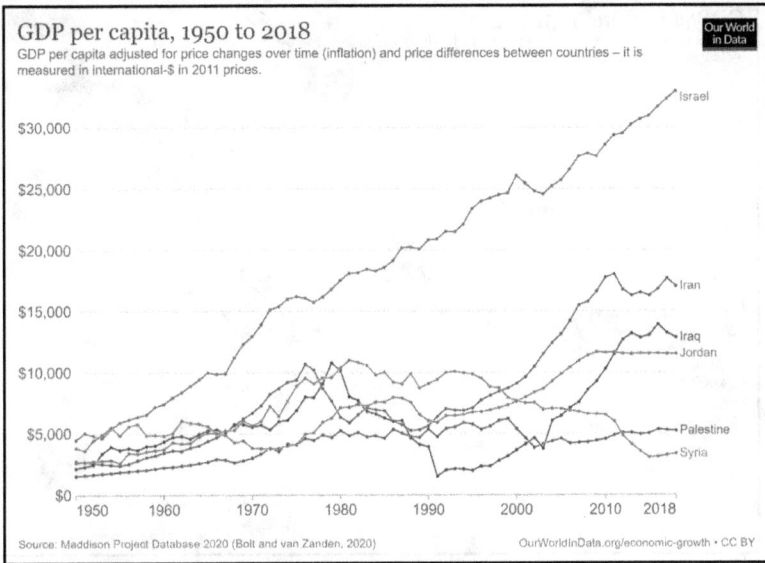

GDP per capita, 1950 to 2018
GDP per capita adjusted for price changes over time (inflation) and price differences between countries – it is measured in international-$ in 2011 prices.

Source: Maddison Project Database 2020 (Bolt and van Zanden, 2020)   OurWorldInData.org/economic-growth • CC BY

Fig. 7   Middle East

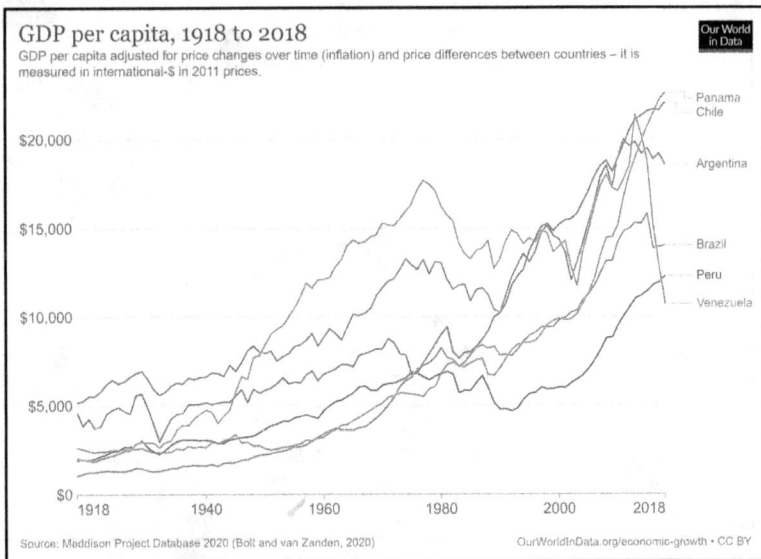

GDP per capita, 1918 to 2018
GDP per capita adjusted for price changes over time (inflation) and price differences between countries – it is measured in international-$ in 2011 prices.

Source: Maddison Project Database 2020 (Bolt and van Zanden, 2020)   OurWorldInData.org/economic-growth • CC BY

Fig. 8   South America

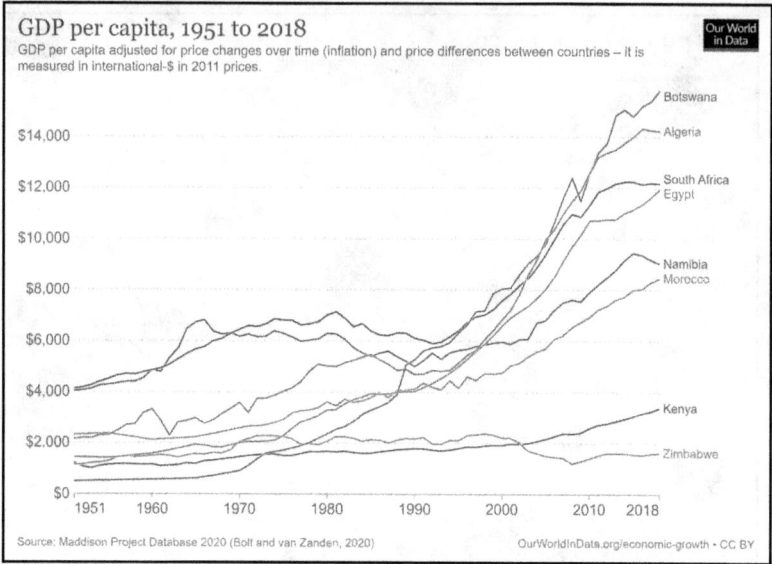

GDP per capita, 1951 to 2018

GDP per capita adjusted for price changes over time (inflation) and price differences between countries — it is measured in international-$ in 2011 prices.

Source: Maddison Project Database 2020 (Bolt and van Zanden, 2020)   OurWorldInData.org/economic-growth · CC BY

Fig. 9   Africa

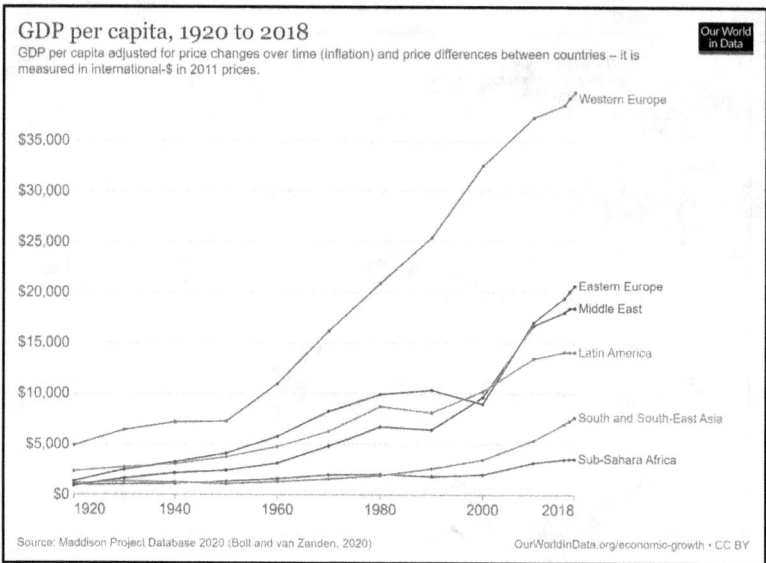

GDP per capita, 1920 to 2018

GDP per capita adjusted for price changes over time (inflation) and price differences between countries — it is measured in international-$ in 2011 prices.

Source: Maddison Project Database 2020 (Bolt and van Zanden, 2020)   OurWorldInData.org/economic-growth · CC BY

Fig. 10   Regions

Permission to use the above graphs has been provided free of charge by Our World in Data.

II

Recommended Reading

Steven Pinker, Enlightenment Now, 2018

If we follow the headlines, the world in the twenty-first century appears to be sinking into chaos, hatred and irrationality. Yet, as Steven Pinker shows, if we follow the trendlines, we discover that our lives have become longer, healthier, safer and more prosperous – not just in developed nations, but worldwide. Such progress is no accident: it's the gift of a coherent value system that many of us embrace without even realising it. These are the values of the Enlightenment: of reason, science, humanism and progress. The challenges we face today are formidable. But the way to deal with them is not to sink into despair or try to lurch back to a mythical, idyllic past; it's to treat them as problems we can solve, as we have solved other problems in the past. This is the case for an Enlightenment newly recharged for the twenty-first century.

Daniel Hannan, Inventing Freedom, 2013

Daniel Hannan tells us how the English-speaking peoples made the modern world.

"The inhabitants of a damp island at the western tip of the Eurasian landmass stumbled upon the idea that the government ought to be subject to the law, not the other way around. The rule of law created security of property and contract, which in turn led to industrialisation and modern capitalism. For the first time in the history of the species, a system grew up that, on the whole, rewarded production better than predation. That system proved to be highly adaptable. It was taken across the oceans by English-speakers, sometimes imposed by colonial administrators, sometimes carried by patriotic settlers. In the old courthouse in Philadelphia, it was distilled into its purest and most sublime form as the U.S. Constitution."[68]

---

68 Hannan, D. (2013). p. 12

Jonah Goldberg, Suicide of the West, 2018

Goldberg argues that authoritarianism, tribalism, identity politics, nationalism and cults of personality are rotting democracies from within. To survive, societies must renew their sense of gratitude for what our civilisation has given us and rediscover our ideals. Suicide is painless, liberty takes work.

Yuval Levin, The Fractured Republic, 2016

Yuval Levin argues that the politics of nostalgia is destroying us. Individualism, dynamism and liberalisation have come at the cost of dwindling solidarity, cohesion and social order. This has left us with more choices in every realm of life, but less security, stability and national unity. Levin calls for the revival of the middle layers of society: families and communities, schools and churches, charities and associations, local governments and markets.

David Kemp, The Land of Dreams, 2018

As the first book in a landmark five-volume Australian Liberalism series, *The Land of Dreams* describes how Australians laid the foundation for one of the world's most successful countries, with unprecedented levels of personal liberty and social equality.

Henry Hazlitt, Economics in One Lesson, 1946/2020

In 1946, Hazlitt expanded on Frédéric Bastiat's *That Which is Seen and That Which is Unseen* to create what is still regarded as the clearest exposition of economics for a lay audience ever written. The Mises Institute published a new edition in 2020.

Saifedean Ammous, *The Bitcoin Standard, 2018*

Ammous elucidates the economic, social, cultural, and political benefits of sound money over unsound money to enable an informed discussion of the potential role Bitcoin could play in the digital economy of the future.

F.A. Hayek, *The Constitution of Liberty, 1960/2011*

Hayek defends the principles of a free society, casting a sceptical eye on the growth of the welfare state and examining the challenges to freedom posed by an ever-expanding government – as well as the corrosive effects on the creation, preservation and utilisation of knowledge.

Ludwig von Mises, *The Best of Ludwig von Mises, 2019*

Jeffrey Tucker has edited a collection of five of Mises's essays, including *Economic Calculation in the Socialist Commonwealth.* Read these before you tackle *Human Action.*

Frédéric Bastiat, *The Best of Frederic Bastiat, 2020*

Brad Devos has edited a collection of five of Bastiat's essays, including *That Which is Seen and That Which is Unseen* and *A Negative Railroad.* If you enjoyed *The Petition of the Candlemakers,* you will love these.

Deirdre McCloskey, *Bourgeois Equality, 2016*

McCloskey believes that it was ideas that drove "trade tested betterment" – the bizarre liberal ideas of equal liberty and dignity for ordinary folk. Commoners were encouraged to have a go, the bourgeoisie took up the Bourgeois Deal, and we were all enriched.

Matt Ridley, The Rational Optimist, *2011*

Ridley takes a positive view and explains how, due to specialisation and exchange, life just gets better and better.

John Mueller, Capitalism, Democracy & Ralph's Pretty Good Grocery, *1999*

Mueller declares that what is true of Garrison Keillor's fictional store, 'Ralph's Pretty Good Grocery', is also true of democracy and capitalism: if you can't find what you want there, you can probably get along without it. This is an entertaining guide filled with thought-provoking ideas.

III

Bibliography

Acemoglu, D. & Robinson, J.A. (2012). *Why Nations Fail: The origins of power, prosperity and poverty*, Profile Books.

Agrawal, V., Cantor, J.H., Sood, N., & Whaley, C.M. (2021). *The Impact of the Covid-19 Pandemic and Policy Responses on Excess Mortality*, National Bureau of Economic Research.

Allen, D.W. (2021). *Covid Lockdown Costs/Benefits: A Critical Assessment of the Literature*, Simon Fraser University.

Ammous, S. (2018). *The Bitcoin Standard*, John Wiley & Sons

Aristotle, (350 BCE). *Nicomachean Ethics, Book II*, Translated by W.D. Ross, The Internet Classics Archive.

Atlas, S.W. (2021). *A Plague upon our House*, Liberatio Protocol.

Bastiat, C.F. (2007). *The Bastiat Collection*, Ludwig von Mises Institute.

Brown, S.L. et. al. (1974). *The Incredible Bread Machine*, World Research, Inc.

Bylund, P. (2006). *How the Welfare State Corrupted Sweden*, Mises Daily, May 31, 2006.

Diamond, J. (1997). *Guns, Germs and Steel*, Chatto & Windus.

Devos, B. ed. (2020). *The Best of Frederic Bastiat*, American Institute for Economic Research.

Drucker, P. (1954/1968). *The Practice of Management*, Pan Books.

Hobbes, T. (1651/2009). *Leviathan*, Oxford World's Classics.

Fenwick, P. (2016). *Liberty at Risk*, Connor Court.

Friedman, M. & Freidman, R. (1980). *Free to Choose*, Macmillan Company of Australia.

Frijters, P., Foster, G. & Baker M. (2021). *The Great Covid Panic*, Brownstone Institute.

Goldberg, J. (2018). *Suicide of the West*, Crown Forum.

Gupta, S., Bhattacharya, J. & Kulldorff, M. (2021). *The Great Barrington Declaration*, https://gbdeclaration.org.

Haidt, J. (2006). *The Happiness Hypothesis: Finding modern truth in ancient wisdom*, Basic Books.

– *(2012). The Righteous Mind: Why good people are divided by politics and religion*, Penguin.

Haidt. J. & Lukianoff, G. *(2018). The Coddling of the American Mind: How good intentions and bad ideas are setting up a generation for failure*, Penguin.

Hannan, D. (2013). *Inventing Freedom: How the English-speaking peoples made the modern world*, HarperCollins Publishers.

Harari, Y. N. (2011). *Sapiens: A brief history of humankind*, Vintage Books.

Hayek, F.A. (1944/2007). *The Road to Serfdom*, University of Chicago Press.

– (1960/2011). *The Constitution of Liberty*, University of Chicago Press.

– (1988). *The Fatal Conceit*, University of Chicago Press.

Hazlitt, H. (1946/2020). *Economics in One Lesson*, Mises Institute.

Hobbes, T. (1651/2009). *Leviathan,* Oxford World's Classics.

Kemp, D. (2018) *The Land of Dreams: How Australians won their freedom*, The Miegunyah Press.

Levin, Y. (2011). *Beyond the Welfare State*, National Affairs, 2011 issue 7.

– (2016). *The Fractured Republic: Renewing America's Social Contract in the Age of Individualism*, Basic Books.

Lindsay, J and Boyle, P. (2017). *The conceptual penis as a social construct*, Cogent Social Sciences.

McCloskey, D.N. (2006). *The Bourgeois Virtues: Ethics for an age of commerce*, University of Chicago Press.

– (2010). *Bourgeois Dignity: Why economics can't explain the modern world*, University of Chicago Press.

– (2016). *Bourgeois Equality: How ideas, not capital or institutions, enriched the world*, University of Chicago Press.

– (2019). *Economical Writing*, University of Chicago Press.

– (1999, 2019). *Crossing: A transgender memoir*, University of Chicago Press.

– (2019). *Why Liberalism Works: How true liberal values produce a freer, more equal, prosperous world for all*, Yale University Press.

– (2020). *The Bourgeois Deal*, University of Chicago Press.

McCloskey, D.N. & Carden, A. (2020). *Leave Me Alone and I'll Make You Rich*, University of Chicago Press.

Mill, J.S. (1859/2003). *On Liberty*, Penguin.

Mises, L. von, (1912/1932). *The Theory of Money and Credit*, Jonathan Cape.

– (1922/1951). *Socialism: An Economic and Sociological Analysis*, Yale University Press.

– (1927/1962). *Liberalism*, D. Van Nostrand.

– (1929/1976). *A Critique of Interventionism*, Arlington House.

– (1933/1960). *Epistemological Problems in Economics*, D. Van Nostrand.

– (1944). *Omnipotent Government: The Rise of the Total State & Total War*, Yale University Press.

– (1944). *Bureaucracy*, Yale University Press.

– (1949). *Human Action*, Yale University Press.

Mueller, J. (1999). *Capitalism, Democracy & Ralph's Pretty Good Grocery*, Princeton Paperbacks.

Murakami, H. (2003). *Norwegian Wood*, Random House.

Murphy, P. (2001). *Civic Justice: From ancient Greece to the modern world*, Prometheus Books.

– *(2012). The Collective Imagination: The creative spirit of free societies*, Routledge.

– *(2015). Universities and Innovation Economies: The creative wasteland of post-industrial societies*, Ashgate.

– *(2017). Auto-industrialism: DIY capitalism and the rise of the auto-industrial society*, Sage Publications.

– *(2019). Limited Government: The public sector in the auto-industrial age*, Routledge.

– *(2020-1). The Political Economy of Prosperity: Successful societies and productive cultures*, Routledge.

– *(2020-2). COVID-19: Proportionality, public policy and social distancing*, Palgrave Pivot.

Newman, J. H. (1853,1858/ 1959). *The Idea of a University*, Image Books.

Palmer, T.G. ed. (2011). *The Morality of Capitalism: What your professors won't tell you*, Jameson Books.

Perrottet, D. (2016). *Deconstructing Greer*, The Spectator, 23 April 2016.

Pinker, S. (2013). *The Better Angels of Our Nature: A history of violence and humanity*, Penguin.

– (2018). *Enlightenment Now: The case for reason, science, humanism and progress,* Allen Lane.

Prins, G. (2021). *The Worm in the Rose,* The Global Warming Policy Forum

Rawls, J. (1996). *Political Liberalism,* Columbia University Press

Ricardo, D. (1817/2004). *Principles of Political Economy and Taxation,* Dover Publications.

Ridley, M. (2010). *The Rational Optimist: How prosperity evolves,* Harper Perennial.

– (1998). *The Origins of Virtue: Human instincts and the evolution of cooperation,* Penguin.

– (2000). *Genome: The autobiography of a species in 23 chapters,* Penguin.

– (2003). *The Red Queen: Sex and the evolution of human nature,* Harper Perennial.

– (2004). *The Agile Gene: How nature turns on nurture,* Harper Perennial.

– (2011). *Francis Crick: Discoverer of the genetic code,* Harper Perennial.

– (2016). *The Evolution of Everything: How new ideas emerge,* Fourth Estate.

– *(2020). How Innovation Works: And why it flourishes in freedom,* Fourth Estate.

Rothbard, M.N., (1963/2005). *What has Government Done to Our Money?,* Ludwig von Mises Institute

– (1963/2013). *America's Great Depression,* Ludwig von Mises Institute.

Saad, G. (2020). *The Parasitic Mind: How infectious ideas are killing common sense,* Regnery Publishing.

Sabhlok, S. (2020). *The Great Hysteria and the Broken State,* Connor Court.

Shlaes, A. (2019). *Great Society: A new history,* Harper Perennial.

Smith, A. (1776/1964). *The Wealth of Nations,* Everyman's Library, J.M. Dent & Sons

Solzhenitsyn, A. (1973/2018). *The Gulag Archipelago,* Vintage Classics

Stockman, D. (2013). *The Great Deformation,* Public Affairs.

Tucker, J. ed. (2019). *The Best of Ludwig von Mises,* American Institute for Economic Research

Wheatley, M.J. (1992/2018). *Leadership and the New Science: Discovering order in a chaotic world*, Berrett-Koehler Publishers.

– (2006). *Finding Our Way: Leadership for an uncertain time*, Berrett-Koehler Publishers.

– (2009). *Turning to One Another: Simple conversations to restore hope for the future*, Berrett-Koehler Publishers.

– (2012). *So Far from Home: Lost and found in our brave new world*, Berrett-Koehler Publishers.

– (2010). *Perseverance*, Berrett-Koehler Publishers.

– (2017). *Who Do We Choose to Be? Facing reality, claiming leadership, restoring sanity*, Berrett-Koehler Publishers.

Wheatley, M.J. & Kellner-Rogers, M. (1996). *A Simpler Way*, Berrett-Koehler Publishers.

Wheatley, M.J. & Frieze, D. (2011). *Walk Out Walk On: A learning journey into communities daring to live the future now*, Berrett-Koehler Publishers.

About the Author

Peter Fenwick was born in Geelong, Victoria and educated at The Geelong College. He studied civil engineering at the Gordon Institute of Technology and The University of Melbourne, graduating in 1966. In 1972 he was awarded a Master of Business Administration with distinction, from The University of Melbourne.

In 1976, Peter founded Fenwick Software, an IT consultancy that implements commercial systems for businesses in the manufacturing, distribution and waste management industries. He established an employee shareholder scheme, and staff now own over 75 per cent. The business is thriving and now has over 40 staff. Greg Galloway has been managing the firm since 2011.

At The University of Melbourne, Peter studied philosophy under the charismatic Father Eric Darcy. He is an alumnus of the Cranlana colloquium, a facilitated program inspired by the Aspen Institute in the United States. Peter's classical liberal scholarship was given practical expression in the culture and practices of his consulting business.

Since retiring, he has continued his interest in the Scottish Enlightenment and Austrian economics. He has written two books, The Fragility of Freedom: Why subsidiarity matters (2014) and Liberty at Risk: Tackling today's political problems (2016), both published by Connor Court. He blogs at www.peterfenwick.com, where he offers insights into contemporary issues.

Peter plays chess and royal tennis. He is a member of the Royal Melbourne Tennis Club. Peter has been married to Jill, a schoolteacher and author, since 1966. They have three sons and three grandchildren. They live in East Melbourne, Australia.

www.ingramcontent.com/pod-product-compliance
Lightning Source LLC
Chambersburg PA
CBHW070338270326
41926CB00017B/3905